THE NEVILLE GODDARD HANDBOOK

NOAH PRESS

CONTENTS

PART I
INTRODUCTION

NEVILLE GODDARD - THE MAGIC MYSTIC

❦

NEVILLE GODDARD REMAINS A TOWERING figure in the field of mysticism and the study of reality creation. His teachings imbued with the wisdom of ancient truths and a profound understanding of the human psyche, have transformed the lives of millions, offering a pathway to personal fulfillment and spiritual enlightenment.

In embarking upon this exploration, we must acquaint ourselves with the man behind the philosophy. Neville Goddard, born into an English family in Barbados in 1905, was the beacon of a unique blend of cultural and spiritual ideologies. His early life on the island, characterized by its stunning landscapes and vibrant culture, shaped his perspectives.

As a young man of only 17, Neville's journey to the United States began a profound transformation. Initially drawn to the arts, he immersed himself in drama and dance, disciplines that no doubt honed his ability to envision and embody varied realities. However, his eventual foray into metaphysics unveiled his true calling. The shift from the performative arts to the introspective realm of spirituality was catalyzed by his exposure to literature on the power of the mind, a topic that would consume his intellectual pursuits henceforth.

Neville's metamorphosis from an aspiring actor to a mystic and philosopher was not without its challenges. In the early 20th century, the study of metaphysics and spirituality outside traditional religious institutions was often met with skepticism, if not outright disdain. Yet, Neville's unyielding curiosity and desire for understanding propelled him forward, guiding him to sources of wisdom that would illuminate his path.

Among Neville's guides, Abdullah, an Ethiopian Rabbi, stood as the most pivotal mentor, profoundly shaping his journey. Abdullah's deep scholarship in Esoteric Christianity and his unique life as a marginalized minority in the US forged him into a figure of immense resilience and wisdom. Despite societal challenges, Abdullah's powerful self-concept and unwavering dignity set him apart, embodying the very principles he taught.

His unconventional approach to scripture, favoring symbolic over literal interpretations, opened vast new realms of thought for Neville. Through Abdullah's guidance, Neville came to see the Bible not merely as a historical account but as a treasure trove of mystical truths. Each biblical story and character, as presented by Abdullah, was a mirror reflecting the inner struggles and triumphs of the human spirit.

Abdullah's influence was unparalleled, casting a long and enriching shadow over Neville's teachings. It was under Abdullah's tutelage that Neville learned to navigate the complexities of spiritual understanding with grace, viewing life's challenges not as obstacles but as opportunities for growth. Through Abdullah, Neville was introduced to a world where every narrative within sacred texts became a guidepost for the soul's journey towards enlightenment.

Abdullah's teachings on the Law of Assumption, a principle asserting the creative power of belief and imagination, became the cornerstone of Neville's philosophy. This law posits that by assuming the reality of your desires, by living and feeling as if they have already come to fruition, you set into motion the forces necessary to manifest those desires in the physical world. It is a principle that echoes across various spiritual traditions, yet Neville's articulation of it, influenced by Abdullah's wisdom, brought it to life for a modern audience.

Neville's dedication to his mentor and to the principles he taught is a testament to the transformative power of guidance and wisdom passed down through generations. As Neville navigated the complexities of metaphysical study, he became a conduit for these teachings, refining and sharing them with an ever-growing audience. His lectures, primarily delivered in New York and Los Angeles throughout the 1960s, drew crowds eager to learn about the

Law of Assumption and to discover the potential within themselves to create their reality.

The essence of Neville's teachings is captured in his reinterpretation of biblical stories and characters as allegories for the spiritual journey of every individual. He argued that these narratives were not historical accounts but symbolic representations of the eternal struggle between man's divine nature and his earthly constraints. This perspective offered a radical reinterpretation of religious texts, inviting believers and skeptics alike to explore the deeper, mystical meanings behind familiar stories.

Neville's influence extended beyond his immediate audience, inspiring future generations of thinkers, writers, and seekers. His ability to distill complex metaphysical concepts into accessible, practical wisdom made his teachings remarkably relevant to a wide range of individuals. Whether one was seeking spiritual enlightenment, personal improvement, or a deeper understanding of the universe's workings, Neville's lectures and writings offered guidance and inspiration.

As we delve deeper into Neville Goddard's life and legacy, we uncover the universal themes that resonate with the human experience across time and culture. His teachings on the Law of Assumption, the symbolic interpretation of scripture, and the divine nature of the individual challenge us to reconsider our perceptions of reality, spirituality, and our potential to shape our destinies.

In reflecting upon Neville's journey and the wisdom he

shared, we are reminded of the profound impact that a single individual can have on the collective consciousness. Through his exploration of mysticism, his reinterpretation of sacred texts, and his unwavering belief in the power of the human imagination, Neville Goddard has left an indelible mark on the world.

As we conclude this introduction to Neville Goddard and his teachings, let us ponder his profound assertion that the external world is but a mirror of our internal state. This principle, encapsulated in his urging to change our self-concept rather than attempting to alter the world around us, serves as a guiding light for all who seek to understand the mysteries of existence and to realize their highest potential.

"The world is a mirror, reflecting our beliefs, our fears, and our divine essence. By altering our perceptions and assumptions, we not only transform our individual lives but contribute to the collective evolution of humanity,"

Neville might say if he were addressing us today. This call to introspection and self-transformation is at the heart of Neville's legacy, a legacy that continues to inspire and empower.

IS THIS BOOK FOR YOU?

NEVILLE GODDARD'S legacy in the realm of manifestation and reality creation remains unparalleled.Even though he has passed beyond the veil of the physical realm, his teachings echo with undiminished power within the manifestation community, their relevance transcending the boundaries of time. Across various platforms, from digital forums to social media, Neville's insights and methodologies occupy a place of honor, illuminating the paths of those who seek to harness the power of their minds.

His work has inspired an abundance of literature, online courses, and even dedicated YouTube channels, all bearing his name and extending his teachings to a global audience. Before embarking on this profound journey through Neville's teachings, it's crucial to pause and reflect on your intentions and aspirations. What do you hope to achieve through this exploration? Whether you're a long-standing admirer of Neville's work or a newcomer to his philosophies, understanding your goals will enhance your engagement with the material and enrich your learning experience.

Consider this book not merely as a collection of lessons but as a journey of transformation. It demands your time and energy, inviting you to delve deep into Neville's world. To fully benefit from this exploration, it is advisable to approach it with clarity and commitment. Engaging actively with the content, perhaps by keeping a dedicated journal, will help you navigate the wealth of information and insights presented.

The act of taking notes is more than a mere academic exercise; it is a crucial strategy for internalizing and retaining the profound principles shared throughout this book. Our brains are wired to strengthen neural pathways through repetition, turning fleeting insights into deep, enduring knowledge.

This journey through Neville Goddard's teachings is open to all—whether you are taking your first steps into the world of manifestation or seeking to deepen your understanding with advanced techniques. For those new to Neville's work, you stand at the threshold of a transformative experience. His teachings offer the keys to unlocking a new realm of possibilities, empowering you to reshape your life through the mastery of your mind.

The book is structured to guide you systematically through the foundational aspects of Neville's philosophy before introducing his more advanced techniques. By starting with the core teachings, we ensure a solid foundation upon which to build a comprehensive understanding of his methods. This structured approach is designed to cater to both beginners and those familiar with Neville's work, ensuring that everyone finds value and depth in the material covered.

As we progress through the book, you will encounter both familiar concepts and new techniques that may surprise you. The objective is to furnish you with a broad spectrum of tools, allowing you to select the methods that resonate most deeply with you.

Manifestation, the art of bringing your desires into reality through the power of your mind, lies at the heart of Neville's teachings. It is a concept that captivates and inspires, promising the ability to craft the life of your dreams. This book is designed with the intention of demystifying the process of manifestation, providing practical guidance and actionable steps to manifest not only wealth but all forms of abundance and success.

By exploring Neville's core teachings, his techniques, and the art of manifestation, you will gain access to a comprehensive framework for creating the life you desire. The book includes a special focus on manifesting wealth, a topic of great interest to many followers of Neville's teachings. Through the Money Manifestation Blueprint, you will discover strategies for attracting financial abundance and creating prosperity.

In addition to the main content, the book offers bonus material for those eager to delve even deeper into the principles of manifestation. This section includes powerful affirmations and guided meditations designed to enhance your manifestation abilities and elevate your practice to new heights.

The universe is a canvas of infinite potential, and you, as an integral part of this magnificent creation, possess the right to achieve all that your heart desires. As you embark on this journey, guided by Neville Goddard's wisdom, you will learn to align your mind with the abundance of the universe, transforming your dreams into reality.

Are you ready to unlock the secrets to an abundant life, filled with all the richness and fulfillment you've ever imagined? Join us as we delve into the teachings of Neville Goddard, embarking on a transformative journey that promises to reshape your reality and unveil the boundless possibilities that await.

PART II
NEVILLE'S CORE TEACHINGS

CONSCIOUS VS. THE SUBCONSCIOUS MIND

❧

"Consciousness is the one and only reality, not figuratively but actually. This reality may for the sake of clarity be likened unto a stream which is divided into two parts, the conscious and the subconscious. In order to intelligently operate the law of consciousness, it is necessary to understand the relationship between the conscious and the subconscious. The conscious is personal and selective; the subconscious is impersonal and non-selective. The conscious is the realm of effect; the subconscious is the realm of cause. These two aspects are the male and female divisions of consciousness. The conscious is male; the subconscious is female. The conscious generates ideas and impresses these ideas on the subconscious; the subconscious receives ideas and gives form and expression to them."
– *Neville Goddard*

This chapter aims to explore the dual nature of

consciousness, the conscious and subconscious mind, and their critical roles in shaping our experiences and realities.

In a world bounded by physical limitations, it's easy to succumb to the notion that our circumstances and bodily constraints dictate the scope of our possibilities. However, such a view overlooks the infinite potential of the human mind. While our physical bodies have their limitations, our minds are free to traverse infinity. They hold the power to transcend the tangible, to imagine, create, and transform our reality in ways beyond our physical capabilities.

The human mind, with its dynamic and limitless nature, stands as the ultimate tool for creation. It is where the seeds of every invention, discovery, and artistic creation first take root before manifesting in the physical world. From the awe-inspiring achievements of human ingenuity to the everyday solutions that simplify life, the origin of all is the imagination.

Neville Goddard elevates the concept of imagination from a mere mental faculty to a divine capability inherent within each of us. He posits that the human imagination is the "true vine of eternity," an eternal body of God that we all possess. This perspective invites us to view our creative potential not just as a personal attribute but as a divine endowment, capable of shaping not only our lives but the world at large.

Yet, if the imagination holds such transformative power, why does suffering persist? Why do so many remain unaware of or unable to utilize this divine gift to shape a better reality for themselves?

The key to unlocking the full potential of our imagination lies in understanding the relationship between the conscious and subconscious aspects of our minds. The conscious mind, characterized by its capacity for logic, reasoning, and selective attention, serves as the gatekeeper to the subconscious. It is in the unconscious mind that ideas are born and nurtured.

The subconscious mind, by contrast, operates beyond the realm of conscious awareness. It does not judge or discriminate but accepts the impressions and ideas seeded by the conscious mind, giving them form and expression. This impersonal and non-selective nature of the subconscious makes it a fertile ground for the manifestation of ideas into reality.

The process of impressing ideas onto the subconscious is critical to their manifestation. It is not enough for an idea to simply exist within the conscious mind; it must be deeply impressed upon the subconscious to take root and grow. This act of impression is akin to planting a seed in fertile soil, where it can germinate and eventually break through into the physical realm.

Understanding this dynamic interaction between the conscious and subconscious mind illuminates the pathway to mastering our reality. It reveals the mechanism through which our thoughts, beliefs, and imaginations translate into the experiences and circumstances of our lives.

Many of us, unbeknownst to ourselves, carry limiting beliefs and negative impressions that have been deeply embedded in our subconscious. These impressions often stem from early life experiences and societal conditioning, shaping our perception of what is possible and holding us back from realizing our full potential.

Neville's teachings offer a framework for identifying, challenging, and transforming these limiting beliefs. By consciously choosing and impressing new, empowering ideas onto our subconscious, we can begin to rewrite the script of our lives, opening ourselves to new possibilities and experiences.

Great minds throughout history, such as Nikola Tesla and many others, have harnessed the power of their subconscious to access insights, innovations, and solutions far beyond the reach of ordinary thought. This ability to tap into the subconscious is not reserved for a select few but is accessible to all who are willing to explore the depths of their consciousness.

Practices such as meditation, visualization, and affirmation can serve as bridges to the subconscious, allowing us to silence the chatter of the conscious mind and access the vast reservoir of creativity, wisdom, and potential that lies within.

As we conclude this exploration of consciousness, let us remember that the power to shape our reality lies within us. Our imagination, a divine faculty, offers us the tools to create, transform, and transcend. By understanding and leveraging the relationship between the conscious and subconscious mind, we can unlock the door to infinite possibilities and step into the life we have always imagined.

In the words of Neville Goddard, nothing is impossible to our wonderful human imagination. Let us, therefore, embrace this divine gift, and with intention and purpose, shape the reality of our dreams.

YOU CAN CHANGE YOUR PAST!

"Do not waste one moment in regret, for to think feelingly of the mistakes of the past is to re-infect yourself. Turn from appearances and assume the feeling that would be yours were you already the one you wish to be."
– Neville Goddard

REFLECTING on Neville Goddard's profound insights thus far, we've come to understand that the tapestry of our reality is intricately woven from the threads of our thoughts, emotions, and beliefs. Life, much like a mirror, merely reflects the internal tumult or tranquility that characterizes our inner being onto the canvas we call our lives. Neville suggests that rather than contesting what is seen in the mirror—a common approach—we should focus on addressing the source of the reflection through introspection. To change our reality, it's essential to delve inward and initiate transformation at the foundation of our consciousness. To alter our reality, we must venture inward, initiating change at the very core of our consciousness.

Take a moment to notice the numerous thoughts crossing your mind. You may come across some thoughts related to the present moment, but most of them will be about the past. Our minds tend to replay past events with great intensity, which often leaves little room for the present or future.

This is because the mind functions as a repository of the past, cataloging experiences along with the resultant emotions and beliefs forged through those experiences. This archival function is crucial, aiding us in navigating life without falling prey to past follies. For instance, consider the profound impact of a painful lesson learned from a childhood burn. Such an experience, though seemingly small, embeds itself deeply within our psyche, serving as a potent, cautionary tale. This burn, perhaps resulting from a moment of youthful curiosity—reaching out to touch a hot stove or the flicker of a candle flame—translates into a vivid memory charged with pain and surprise. The immediate physical pain of the burn is accompanied by an emotional realization: the world contains elements that can harm us if we are not careful.

This lesson extends far beyond the initial incident. It imprints a cautionary blueprint in our minds, steering us away from similar harm in the future. The memory of the burn becomes a subconscious reminder of the importance of assessing risks and being mindful of our surroundings. This does not mean we live in fear, but rather with a heightened awareness of our actions and their potential consequences.

Moreover, this childhood experience of a burn teaches us about resilience and recovery. The pain eventually subsides, and the wound heals, showing us our body's remarkable ability to recover and adapt. This cycle of action, consequence, and recovery serves as a foundational lesson in cause and effect, shaping our approach to new experiences and challenges as we grow.

Thus, a simple yet painful incident, like a childhood burn, encompasses a multitude of lessons—caution, awareness, resilience, and the natural laws of cause and effect. It underscores the complex way in which early experiences shape our understanding of the world and influence our behavior long into adulthood.

However, this protective mechanism morphs into a double-edged sword when our perception of reality becomes so tinted by past experiences that we close ourselves off to new possibilities. Past heartbreaks, failures, or losses should not define our openness to love, success, or joy in the present and future. Yet, the survival brain, in its quest to shield us from pain, often traps us in a loop of past memories, stifling growth and transformation.

If we wish to master our destinies and craft our realities, we cannot afford to dwell incessantly in the past. Embracing beliefs anchored in past experiences only serves to recreate similar circumstances, contrary to the essence of reality creation. Given that time is an illusion, with the past, present, and future existing simultaneously in the infinite now, the present moment stands as the fertile ground for creation. It is here, in the present, that we have the power to seed new emotions and forge a destiny anew.

However, breaking free from the shackles of past thoughts and emotions is no simple feat. Our minds, having grown accustomed to familiar patterns of thinking, resist venturing into the unknown, preferring the comfort of the known, however limiting it may be. Neville Goddard, with his mystic insight, recognized this human predicament: our attachment to the past hinders our ability to envision and create a different future.

Dr. Joe Dispenza, a renowned neuroscientist celebrated for his work on the mind-body connection, elaborates on this phenomenon, illustrating how our bodies and minds become addicted to familiar emotions, trapping us in a cycle of negative thinking and feeling. He elucidates:

"Most people are constantly reaffirming their emotional states. So, when it comes time to give up that emotion, they can say I really want to do it. But their body and mind have memorized those emotional states so well that they cannot help but feel the same way again and again. The servant now has become the master and the person, all of a sudden, once they step into that unknown, they'd rather feel guilt and suffering because at least they can predict it. Being in the unknown is a scary place for most people because the unknown is uncertain."

The reality creation equation states that our thoughts and emotions shape our mood and manifest as external circumstances. Thus, a persistent negative mood is likely to cultivate a life marred by negativity, reflecting the alignment between our inner and outer worlds.

Neville Goddard's teachings often emphasize the transformative power of revision—a technique that allows us to alter our past in our minds, thereby influencing our present and future. A particularly poignant application of this technique is in the realm of healing childhood experiences. Many of us carry wounds from childhoods that, in reality or our perception, lacked love, connection, and nurturing. By revisiting these memories with the intention of infusing them with the qualities they missed, we can significantly impact our current emotional wellbeing and relationships.

Consider an individual, let's call her Emma, who reflects on her childhood as being devoid of warmth and affection. Her memories are colored by feelings of isolation and misunderstanding, which have cascaded into her adult life, shaping her self-esteem, her interactions with others, and her ability to form healthy relationships. Guided by Goddard's teachings, Emma embarks on a journey of revision, targeting these critical memories that have contributed to her sense of unworthiness and disconnection.

Emma selects a particularly poignant memory—a birthday where she felt most alone, with no one to share in her joy or understand her desires. In the revision process, she closes her eyes and reimagines the scene. But this time, she visualizes it infused with love and attention. In her revised memory, her family and friends gather around her, their faces alight with joy and affection. She hears their laughter, feels the warmth of their hugs, and sees the genuine love in their eyes. They celebrate not just her birthday, but her, acknowledging her worth, her desires, and her importance in their lives.

This act of revising her memory is not about denying the pain or pretending it never happened. Instead, it's a powerful exercise in reshaping her emotional landscape. By mentally altering the narrative of her past, Emma begins to shift her internal dialogue from one of lack and unworthiness to one of love and belonging. This shift does not occur overnight, but with consistent practice, Emma notices a gradual transformation in how she perceives herself and interacts with the world around her.

The magic of this revision technique lies in its ability to rewrite the emotional scripts that have dictated our lives. By changing the story of her childhood from one of neglect to one of nurturing, Emma not only heals old wounds but also opens herself up to a present and future filled with deeper connections and self-love. Her relationships start to reflect this new narrative, becoming more profound and meaningful. She finds herself more open to love, better able to express her needs, and more resilient in the face of challenges.

Dr. Dispenza's assertion that we often misremember our past, alongside research suggesting that our memories are malleable and influenced by our current emotional state, underscores the potential for revision as a transformative tool. This technique allows us to actively reshape our past, altering its influence on our present and future.

Neville emphasizes the importance of forgiveness as a component of revision. Forgiving ourselves, others, and the circumstances that caused us pain frees us from the chains of the past, enabling us to craft a new future. He asserts:

"Revision is of greatest importance when the motive is to change oneself, when there is a sincere desire to be something different, when the longing is to awaken the ideal active spirit of forgiveness. Without imagination, man remains a being of sin. Man, either goes forward to imagination or remains imprisoned in his senses. To go forward to imagination is to forgive. Forgiveness is the life of the imagination. The art of living is the art of forgiving. Forgiveness is, in fact, experiencing in imagination the revised version of the day, experiencing in imagination what you wish you had experienced in the flesh. Every time one really forgives – that is, every time one relives the event as it should have been lived – one is born again."

THUS, to navigate towards the life we desire, we must first address and revise our past. Holding onto unresolved trauma from our past not only hinders our present but also shapes our future in its image. The present moment offers us the canvas to create anew, to paint a masterpiece with the palette of our desires, dreams, and aspirations. Why, then, should we allow the past to dictate the strokes of our brush?

Embracing forgiveness, both of ourselves and others, marks the first step towards liberation from the past. Making the conscious decision to not let the past define our present and future is the essence of taking responsibility for our lives. As we do so, the universe aligns, providing us with the resources to excel and thrive.

As we conclude this exploration of Neville Goddard's teachings on the power of revising the past and embracing forgiveness, we are reminded of the transformative potential that lies within each of us. Through conscious effort, we can transcend the limitations of our past experiences, opening the door to a future filled with infinite possibilities.

YOUR FEELINGS CREATE YOUR REALITY

AT THE HEART of Neville Goddard's philosophy lies a profound truth: the creation of our reality is intricately tied to the interplay between our thoughts and emotions. Goddard asserts that while thoughts are the mold, it is our feelings that breathe life into our desires, transforming them from mere thought-forms into tangible experiences. This chapter delves into the essence of this process, guiding us on how to harness our feelings to consciously shape our lives.

Every day, our minds are abuzz with thousands of thoughts, but it is the emotional charge behind these thoughts that holds the power to alter our reality. Thoughts themselves are like seeds, neutral and potential-filled. It is the feelings they evoke—their vibrational energy—that determine whether these seeds will flourish or fade.

Goddard's teachings challenge us to go beyond mere positive thinking, inviting us to delve deeper into the realm of emotion. He proposes that the true alchemy of manifestation doesn't occur at the level of the mind but within the crucible of the heart. Our feelings, he argues, are the true architects of our reality.

"Assume the feeling of the wish fulfilled,"

Goddard advises. This simple directive underscores the methodology of manifesting desires according to his teachings. To bring a desire into reality, one must inhabit the emotional state as if the wish is already achieved. This means embracing the joy, contentment, and gratitude you anticipate feeling in the fulfillment of your desire, here and now, before any physical evidence of it appears.

Consider the desire for a new career opportunity. It's insufficient to merely think positively about obtaining such a position. According to Goddard, one should immerse themselves in the feeling state associated with already having this job. This involves engaging in the emotional experience of contributing your skills in a meaningful way, feeling the satisfaction of accomplishing tasks, and the joy of being part of a team that values your contributions. This emotional rehearsal is not just a practice of hopeful thinking but a deliberate act of creation.

The transformation of our reality through the mastery of our emotional states necessitates a heightened level of self-awareness and mindfulness. Meditation offers a powerful tool in this quest, providing a refuge from the constant stream of thoughts and allowing us to consciously select which emotions we wish to cultivate and manifest in our lives.

Through meditation, we gain the ability to quiet the mind and focus on our desired feelings, nurturing them until they become our dominant emotional state. This practice is instrumental in influencing the subconscious mind, which acts as a faithful servant to the conscious mind's emotional directives. By consistently aligning our feelings with those of our desired outcomes, we instruct the subconscious to manifest these outcomes in our external world.

Goddard's insights into the manifestation process remind us that our feelings are not passive reactions to the circumstances of our lives but active tools of creation. By deliberately choosing and embodying the feelings associated with our desired states, we initiate a powerful process of transformation. This process, grounded in the emotional reality of our wishes fulfilled, compels the universe to materialize our desires in the physical realm.

The teachings of Neville Goddard present a clear and actionable pathway toward conscious creation. By understanding and applying the principle that our feelings are the driving force behind the manifestation of our desires, we unlock the potential to deliberately shape our reality. This journey into the power of emotion not only enriches our understanding of manifestation but also empowers us to become architects of our destiny, crafting a life that resonates with our deepest aspirations.

Through the practice of embodying our desired feelings,

we engage in a sacred act of co-creation with the universe. This act transcends the limitations of the material world, opening us to a realm of infinite possibility where our heartfelt desires become our lived reality. As we master the art of feeling our desires into existence, we realize the profound potential within us to manifest a life of abundance, joy, and fulfillment—a testament to the transformative power of our emotions.

PERSIST. PERSIST. PERSIST!

"Man fails to do the works of Jesus Christ because he attempts to accomplish them from his present level of consciousness. You will never transcend your present accomplishments through sacrifice and struggle.
Your present level of consciousness will only be transcended as you drop the present state and rise to a higher level. You rise to a higher level of consciousness by taking your attention away from your present limitations and placing it upon that which you desire to be. Do not attempt this in day-dreaming or wishful thinking but in a positive manner. Claim yourself to be the thing desired. I AM that no sacrifice, no diet, no human tricks. All that is asked of you is to accept your desire. If you dare claim it, you will express it."
– Neville Goddard

In the profound teachings of Neville Goddard, we find a cornerstone principle that fundamentally alters our approach to manifesting our desires and transcending our current realities. Goddard posits that our present level of consciousness—shaped by our accumulated beliefs, thoughts, and emotions—sets the boundaries of our achievements. To surpass these limitations, one must not rely on sacrifice or struggle but rather on elevating to a higher state of consciousness. This elevation is achieved by shifting our focus from our current limitations to the embodiment of our desires.

At the heart of conscious creation lies the challenge and necessity to persist in our assumptions until they solidify into tangible reality. Our assumptions about ourselves, others, and the world sculpt our experiences and manifest as physical facets of our lives, embodying our deepest desires. However, between the inception of an intention and its crystallization into our living reality, there exists a temporal buffer—a period that tests our patience and resolve, often leading many to abandon their creative endeavors prematurely.

This temporal lag between desire and manifestation, while disheartening to some, is a fundamental aspect of the manifestation process. It necessitates a departure from the instant gratification we are accustomed to, urging us to embrace patience, mental reprogramming, and the reframing of past experiences. The rewards of such efforts, however, are boundless, empowering us to become architects of our destiny, transcending the role of mere spectators to our circumstances.

Consider the analogy of a gardener planting a seed; this act, though simple, requires deliberate effort and patience.

The process of manifesting one's reality is akin to gardening —it demands attention, care, and time. Our minds, if left untended, become overgrown with the weeds of limiting beliefs and past traumas. The practice of meditation and the deliberate clearing of these mental obstructions prepare the soil of our minds, making it receptive to the seeds of our desires.

Neville emphasizes the importance of this mental preparation through the practice of "Revision" — a technique aimed at reimagining and transforming past experiences to align with our desired state of being. Once our mental ground is fertile and free of the weeds of the past, we can sow the seeds of our desires with confidence.

The gardener does not expect immediate growth; similarly, we must allow time for our desires to germinate and flourish. Doubt and impatience serve only to disrupt this natural process. Neville warns against the destructive power of doubt:

"Doubt is the only force capable of disturbing the seed or impression; to avoid a miscarriage of so wonderful a child, walk in secrecy through the necessary interval of time that it will take the impression to become an expression. Tell no man of your spiritual romance. Lock your secret within you in joy, confident and happy that someday you will bear the son of your lover by expressing and possessing the nature of your impression. Then will you know the mystery of 'God said, let us make man in our image.'"

Persistence in our assumption, devoid of the shadow of

doubt, is the key to unlocking the manifestation of our desires. This unwavering faith must be maintained despite the apparent contradictions presented by our current reality. To rest in the knowledge that our desires are on the verge of materialization is to observe the Sabbath—the divine rest following the completion of creative work.

Neville elucidates the symbolic nature of the Sabbath, not as a literal day of rest but as a metaphorical space wherein we rest in the assurance of our creative endeavors:

"Six days shall work be done, but on the seventh day there shall be to you a holy day, a Sabbath of rest to the Lord."
– Exodus 35:2

This period of rest is not an invitation to idleness but a sacred interval of faith and anticipation, where we maintain a serene confidence in the impending physical manifestation of our desires. Failing to enter this rest signifies an incomplete impression of our desires upon our subconscious, leading to unease and doubt about the outcome.

PART III

NEVILLE'S TECHNIQUES

THE LADDER TECHNIQUE

NEVILLE GODDARD'S teachings intricately weave the concept of the imaginative faculty, embodied by the disciple Bartholomew, as a pivotal force in transcending the average human experience. This faculty, when awakened and disciplined, distinguishes an individual, elevating them above the masses and illuminating their path like a beacon in a world shrouded in darkness. Goddard elucidates this transformative power:

"The sixth disciple is called Bartholomew. This quality is the imaginative faculty, which quality of the mind when once awake distinguishes one from the masses. An awakened imagination places the one so awakened head and shoulders above the average man, giving him the appearance of a beacon light in a world of darkness. No quality so separates man from man as does the disciplined imagination. This is the separation of the wheat from the chaff. Those who have given most to

society are our artists, scientists, inventors, and others with vivid imaginations."

A key aspect of conscious creation, according to Goddard, is the persistence in one's assumption until it manifests into reality. Our beliefs and assumptions about ourselves and the world not only influence our lives but also crystallize into our physical reality. This manifestation process depends on the ability to maintain faith, especially during the temporal delays between intention and its realization.

The journey of manifestation involves a period of waiting that tests the fortitude of our faith and patience. This temporal buffer, often seen as an obstacle, is actually crucial for the maturation of our desires into their physical form. Unlike the societal norm of instant gratification, the nature of manifestation unfolds over time and is founded on belief in the unseen.

Introducing the ladder technique, Neville Goddard offers a practical experiment to demonstrate the power of the subconscious mind and to reinforce our belief in its capabilities. This technique is designed not only to showcase the subconscious mind's influence but also to provide a foundational experience of intentionally impressing a specific desire upon our deeper consciousness.

The ladder experiment involves a two-part practice:

- **Nightly Visualization:** Before going to sleep, visualize

THE NEVILLE GODDARD HANDBOOK

yourself climbing a ladder. Engage all your senses in this visualization. Feel the texture of the ladder, imagine the motion of climbing, and see yourself reaching the top. This visualization should be performed as you drift off to sleep, during the state akin to sleep (SATS), allowing for a deep impression of this action on your subconscious mind.

• **Daytime Affirmations:** During the day, affirm the opposite intention by repeatedly telling yourself, "I will NOT climb a ladder." This creates a conscious counterintention, setting the stage for a demonstration of the subconscious mind's power over conscious thoughts and affirmations.

Goddard's rationale for this approach is to illustrate the subconscious mind's ability to manifest desires, regardless of conscious counteractions. This experiment serves as a profound lesson in the power of the subconscious: once a desire is deeply impressed upon it, the manifestation is inevitable, subject only to the right timing.

The essence of the ladder experiment is to emphasize the importance of persistence in one's assumption without doubt. Goddard cautions against the destructive nature of doubt and highlights the necessity of maintaining secrecy and joy in one's spiritual quest towards realization.

"**Doubt is the only force capable of disturbing the seed or impression; to avoid a miscarriage of so wonderful a child, walk in secrecy through the necessary interval of time that it will take the impression to become an expression. Tell no man of your spiritual romance. Lock**

your secret within you in joy, confident and happy that someday you will bear the son of your lover by expressing and possessing the nature of your impression. Then will you know the mystery of 'God said, let us make man in our image.'"

The ladder experiment not only showcases the profound influence of the subconscious mind but also clarifies the true nature of affirmations. It teaches that the subconscious does not process negations; it focuses on the core subject of the affirmation, reinforcing the intended action or state.

This method acts as a powerful demonstration of the efficacy of imagination and belief in the manifestation process. It underlines a principal teaching of Neville Goddard: once a desire is vividly impressed upon the subconscious, its physical manifestation is assured. Through the discipline of our imagination and unwavering faith, we can navigate the journey of manifesting our deepest aspirations, embracing the transformative potential within us all.

SATS

Embarking upon the journey of mastering the State Akin to Sleep (SATS) as introduced by Neville Goddard offers a profound method for manifesting one's deepest desires. This technique transcends the ordinary boundaries of consciousness by leveraging the liminal space between wakefulness and sleep, effectively serving as a bridge to the subconscious mind. Here, in this fertile ground, the seeds of aspiration find their most potent potential for germination and growth, allowing for the seamless impression of desires onto the fabric of our reality.

The essence of engaging effectively with SATS lies in cultivating a conducive state of consciousness—a dreamlike, drowsy awareness that blurs the lines between the physical world and the imaginal realm. This unique state, described by Goddard, is not merely a threshold to sleep but rather a richly fertile terrain for the sowing of one's desires. Achieving this state necessitates a deliberate winding down of both body and mind, a task that requires finesse and

balance; too much alertness may resist the desired imprcs-
sion, whereas excessive drowsiness may lead to falling
asleep prematurely, bypassing the opportunity for impression entirely.

The process of initiating SATS, according to Goddard,
can be likened to entering a sacred, inner sanctum where
the conscious mind gracefully yields to the deeper, more
profound wisdom of the subconscious. Within this quietude
and stillness, one is invited to perform the imaginal act—to
vividly experience the scene of the desire fulfilled.
Goddard's advocacy for this practice finds its roots in
ancient scriptures, which affirm the divine nature of dreams
and visions as channels for divine instruction:

**"In a dream, in the vision of the night, when deep sleep
falleth on men, in slumberings upon the bed, then he
opens the ears of men and seals the instructions."**

To embark upon the SATS practice, it is imperative to
ensure an environment free from distractions, preparing
both body and mind for the inward journey that awaits. The
ritual of deep, conscious breathing not only facilitates relaxation but also serves as a signal of departure from the external, material world, ushering the practitioner into a state of
heightened inner awareness. The success of this prepara-
tory phase is signified by a profound immersion into the
imaginal realm, where the tangible boundaries of the material world begin to dissolve, leaving behind only the vivid
landscapes of the mind.

Within the sanctified confines of SATS, the individual is tasked with constructing a scene that encapsulates the essence of their desire's fulfillment. This scene, rich with sensory detail and emotional depth, becomes the medium through which the desired state is impressed upon the subconscious. The scene's emotional resonance—how it feels and the reality it suggests—is paramount. It's about embodying the emotion and the state of the wish fulfilled.

Post-visualization, the practitioner is gently guided into sleep, maintaining the emotional resonance of the imaginal act. This ensures that the subconscious continues to process and marinate in the essence of the desired reality, laying the groundwork for its manifestation in the physical world.

Despite the profound potential of SATS, practitioners, especially beginners, might encounter challenges such as difficulty entering the desired state, maintaining focus, or transitioning into sleep afterward. These initial hurdles, though daunting, can be overcome with persistence and dedicated practice. Over time, SATS becomes an integral part of one's nightly routine, transforming into a sacred ritual that opens the doorway to deliberate creation.

Neville Goddard's personal experience of manifesting his journey to Barbados using SATS stands as a testament to the efficacy of this practice. Facing financial constraints and the seemingly impossible dream of returning to his home-land, Goddard, under the mentorship of Abdullah, embarked on a practice of embodying the state of his wish fulfilled—being in Barbados. Night after night, he visualized this reality, persisting despite the absence of immediate external changes.

On a fateful October evening, Neville's conversation with Abdullah catalyzed this journey. Expressing his longing to return to Barbados, Abdullah's assurance, "You are in Barbados," challenged Neville to adopt this reality mentally. Despite initial skepticism, Neville immersed himself in the sensory experience of being in Barbados, embodying the state of the wish fulfilled night after night.

Despite apparent stagnation, a letter from Neville's brother miraculously offered him a ticket to Barbados. Abdullah's unwavering conviction, "You went to Barbados, and you went First Class," materialized when Neville was unexpectedly upgraded to first-class, affirming the profound efficacy of SATS.

This serendipitous event not only physically transported Neville to Barbados but also affirmed living in the wish fulfilled state's profound efficacy. It highlighted SATS's transformative potential, demonstrating its capacity to reshape reality in alignment with our deepest yearnings.

This narrative serves as a beacon of hope and inspiration for those embarking on their manifestation journey. It illustrates the essence of SATS—a technique that transcends mere visualization to foster a deep-seated belief in the inevitability of one's desires. Through Goddard's story, we witness the alchemy of belief and imagination, underscoring the principle that our external world is a reflection of our internal state.

Integrating this profound insight into our SATS practice invites us on a transformative journey, empowering us with the knowledge that our desires are not mere figments of our imagination but seeds of potentiality awaiting realization in the fertile ground of our subconscious. This story, resonant with Goddard's teachings, acts as both a guide and an inspiration, reminding us that the art of manifestation is an inward journey of faith, persistence, and imaginative embodiment. Through the lens of Neville's experience, we are encouraged to harness the creative power of our imaginations, to live in the joyous anticipation of our desires' fulfillment, and to trust in the transformative power of SATS to manifest the life we dare to imagine.

LIVING IN THE END

✤

"Living in the End," as illuminated by Neville Goddard, is a practice of embodying the fulfilled state of your desires, thereby transforming your reality through the potent force of your imagination. This concept is not merely a manifestation technique but a profound shift in consciousness, where you operate from the conviction that your aspiration is already realized in your present reality.

Goddard's philosophy underscores the omnipotence of the imagination and its direct influence on the fabric of our lives. By "Living in the End," you actively engage this creative power, aligning your internal state with the external manifestation of your desires. It's a call to inhabit the emotional landscape of your fulfilled wishes, making it a lived reality even before it materializes physically. This act of faith and imagination is the cornerstone of Goddard's teachings, emphasizing that reality conforms to the contours of our internal states.

This method challenges practitioners to steadfastly maintain the state of their wish fulfilled, despite the current absence of its physical counterpart. It's an invitation to step into a reality where your desires are not future hopes but present facts. By doing so, you not only alter your psychological state but also set in motion the forces that concretize this state in the physical realm.

To effectively "Live in the End," one must first achieve absolute clarity on what is desired. This clarity is crucial because it serves as the foundation upon which the imaginal act is constructed. Following this, the practitioner is encouraged to craft a vivid, sensory-rich scenario where the desire is not only achieved but is being experienced in the now. This scenario should engage all senses to such a degree that the subconscious mind— the fertile ground where seeds of belief take root—cannot distinguish it from physical reality.

Engaging the subconscious mind is pivotal, as it plays a crucial role in the manifestation process. It operates beyond the realm of logic and reason, responding instead to the language of emotions and images. By impressing upon it a vivid and emotionally charged depiction of the desired state, the subconscious begins to align the practitioner's external circumstances with this new reality. This alignment is not random but a direct consequence of the subconscious mind's power to manifest according to the beliefs and images held within it.

Furthermore, "Living in the End" necessitates a transformation in one's self-perception. It requires embodying the identity of the person who has already realized their desire. This might involve adopting new behaviors, attitudes, and even thought patterns that resonate with the reality of the wish fulfilled. This change in self-perception is crucial because it reinforces the imaginal act, making the assumed state not just a practice but a lived experience.

The efficacy of this technique is illustrated through various success stories shared by Goddard, including his own experience of manifesting a trip to Barbados against all odds. Under the guidance of his mentor, Abdullah, Goddard was taught to firmly inhabit the state of being in Barbados, despite the physical and financial constraints suggesting otherwise. His unwavering commitment to this state eventually led to the physical manifestation of his desire, showcasing the remarkable power of living from the end.

Another compelling story shared by Goddard involves a woman, referred to here as Lily, who overcame a seemingly insurmountable challenge through "Living in the End." After years of hard work and dedication, Lily had finally made her apartment a reflection of her personal journey and achievements. Every piece of furniture, every painting, and every decoration was carefully chosen, imbuing her space with memories and meaning. However, her world turned upside down when she returned home one day to find her apartment stripped of its furnishings. The culprit? Her trusted maid, who had disappeared without a trace, along with all of Lily's cherished possessions.

Devastated and feeling betrayed, Lily initially sought to rectify the situation through conventional means. She filed a police report, posted notices, and even reached out to acquaintances in hopes of recovering her belongings. But as days turned into weeks with no progress, Lily's hope began to dwindle.

In her moment of despair, she remembered the teachings of Neville Goddard, which she had once practiced but drifted away from in the hustle and bustle of daily life. Recalling Goddard's emphasis on the power of imagination and living in the end, Lily decided to shift her approach. Instead of focusing on her loss and the betrayal, she began envisioning her apartment restored to its former glory.

Each night before falling asleep, Lily would close her eyes and vividly imagine walking through her apartment. She felt the soft rug beneath her feet, admired the vibrant colors of the paintings on the walls, and sunk into her cozy, plush sofa, feeling the fabric under her fingers. She filled her vision with laughter and warmth, hosting friends in her beautifully restored living space. With every imagined detail, she infused feelings of relief, joy, and satisfaction, truly embodying the state of her wish fulfilled.

The transformation didn't happen overnight, but Lily persisted, nurturing her vision with unwavering faith. Then, one day, an unexpected call from a distant relative turned the tides. They had stumbled upon a collection of furniture and belongings remarkably similar to Lily's at a local auction, being sold under suspicious circumstances. Armed with this information, Lily was able to work with the authorities to trace the items back to a storage unit rented by her former maid.

Thanks to her relentless optimism and the vividness of her imagination, Lily's apartment was gradually restored. Not only did she recover most of her possessions, but the entire experience also led to newfound friendships and support from her community, who rallied around her during the recovery process. This journey, sparked by a leap of faith into the teachings of Neville Goddard, underscored the profound impact of visualization and living in the end. Lily's story became a testament to the power of imagination not just in overcoming material loss, but in transforming adversity into an opportunity for growth and deeper connections.

"Living in the End" is a testament to the transformative potential of our imagination and faith. It invites us to a deeper understanding of our creative power and offers a method to harness this power deliberately. Through consistent practice, emotional engagement, and unwavering belief in the reality of our desires, we can navigate the bridge from desire to manifestation, proving to ourselves that the limits of our reality are as boundless as the reaches of our imagination.

ISN'T IT WONDERFUL?

NEVILLE GODDARD'S "Isn't it Wonderful?" technique unveils a manifestation method tailored for those who might find visualization challenging or seek an alternative approach. This technique stands out for its simplicity and broad applicability, allowing practitioners to address multiple desires simultaneously with an affirming mantra that shifts focus from current limitations to the joy of fulfilled desires.

Goddard's teachings emphasize that our imagination and emotions shape our external reality. Traditionally, many of us condition our happiness on the manifestation of specific desires, not realizing that this perspective inadvertently reinforces a state of lack. The "Isn't it Wonderful?" technique inversely proposes that one must first cultivate an internal state of happiness and contentment to manifest desires into reality. It's a call to embody the emotions associated with having one's desires fulfilled even before they materialize physically.

Neville emphasizes the importance of adopting a proactive stance in shaping our reality:

"You rise to a higher level of consciousness by taking your attention away from your present limitations and placing it upon that which you desire to be. Do not attempt this in day-dreaming or wishful thinking but in a positive manner. Claim yourself to be the thing desired. I AM that no sacrifice, no diet, no human tricks. All that is asked of you is to accept your desire. If you dare claim it, you will express it."

The essence of this technique is encapsulated in a transformative story Neville shared about a 55-year-old woman facing dire financial and personal crises.

In the heart of New York, lived a woman of 55, whose life had become a tapestry of financial strain and emotional desolation. This period of her life was marked by a series of cascading challenges: unemployment that stretched out like a vast, barren field, the mounting pressure of unpaid rent and looming bills, and an aching void where support from family and friends should have been. Her reality was a jigsaw puzzle with pieces that didn't just fail to fit—they were crumbling one after the other.

Despite the shadows that clung to her days, there was a flicker of light—she had been attending Neville Goddard's lectures, where the seeds of a different way of seeing and being in the world were sown. Within these teachings, she found a beacon of hope, the knowledge that the fabric of reality could be woven anew with the threads of imagination. Determined to change her circumstances, she set out to manifest her desires one by one. But the sheer magnitude of what she needed to change was overwhelming, taxing her mental and emotional reserves beyond their limits.

Amidst this tumult of desperation and weariness, a lifeline emerged from the depths of her memory—a technique Neville had once spoken of, a method so simple yet profound in its potential to transform: the "Isn't it wonderful?" technique. It was a beacon in her storm, a way to cast a wide net over her multitude of desires without succumbing to the strain of detailed visualization for each.

With a heart heavy yet hopeful, she began her practice. Night after night, as the city that never sleeps hummed and buzzed beyond her walls, she whispered to herself, "Isn't it wonderful that something marvelous is happening to me now?". This mantra became her shield and sword, her declaration of faith in a reality unseen but deeply felt. With each repetition, a subtle shift began to take root within her; her mood lightened, a sense of satisfaction and peace enveloped her, and the dire state of her current existence began to fade in the light of an unfolding miracle.

For two relentless months, this was her ritual. Each day's end found her reaffirming her belief in the wonderful happenings she was yet to see, a practice she clung to with a tenacity born of having nothing left to lose. Her perseverance was her testament to the belief in Neville's teachings, her unwavering commitment to see her life transformed through the power of her own imagination.

Then, the universe began to weave its magic. A chance encounter with an old friend, whom she had not seen for years, became the first thread of change. This friend, visiting New York, became a guest in her life's narrative, unknowingly set to play a pivotal role. A mere few days after their meeting, a check for 2500 dollars arrived in her mailbox, a gift from this friend, a gesture of kindness that was as unexpected as it was desperately needed.

But the universe wasn't done with her yet. This old friend, through a serendipitous conversation, connected with another of her acquaintances from 25 years past. This man, upon hearing of her plight, decided to extend his generosity in a manner that would secure her financial stability for the immediate future—he committed to sending her monthly checks for two years.

Her world, once darkened by the shadows of scarcity and despair, was now alight with the abundance and warmth of unexpected generosity. The technique she had so faithfully practiced had not only eased her financial burdens but had also rekindled her belief in the goodness of people and the power of the universe to conspire in her favor. Her rent was paid, her car fixed, her loans addressed, and her daily existence secured—all without the immediate need for employment.

This story, a testament to the "Isn't it Wonderful?" technique, illustrates not just a method for manifesting desires but also a profound shift in perspective. It teaches us that by embodying the feeling of our desires being fulfilled, we open ourselves up to receiving the abundance the universe has to offer. It underscores the principle that our inner state is a powerful magnet for our outer reality, and by choosing to dwell in a state of wonder and gratitude, we invite miraculous transformations into our lives.

For those inspired to apply this technique in their own lives, the approach is straightforward yet profound. As you prepare for rest at the end of each day, allow yourself to bask in the feeling that all your worries have dissolved, and every desire is on the verge of manifestation. Whisper to yourself, "Isn't it wonderful that something marvelous is happening to me right now?" Let this affirmation be your lullaby, carrying you into sleep with a heart full of expectation and a spirit buoyed by faith.

Persist in this practice, night after night, and watch as your life begins to unfold in ways you never imagined. The "Isn't it Wonderful?" technique is not just a method but a way of life, a constant reminder that within every moment lies the potential for something truly marvelous

What makes the "Isn't it Wonderful?" technique particularly appealing is its universality and ease of implementation. Without the need to focus on individual desires, this single, powerful affirmation acts as a blanket statement of faith and expectation, covering all areas of need. It simplifies the manifestation process, making it accessible to everyone, regardless of their proficiency with visualization or their familiarity with metaphysical practices.

As we integrate this technique into our daily routines, it's crucial to remember the significance of persistence and emotional investment. The transformative journey of manifestation is not a passive process but an active engagement with our desires, fueled by unwavering faith and a joyful anticipation of the good already unfolding in our lives. Through the "Isn't it Wonderful?" technique, we are reminded of the simplicity and power that lies in gratitude and positive expectation, principles that can guide us toward a life filled with manifested desires and boundless joy.

I REMEMBER WHEN!

DIVING into the essence of Neville Goddard's transformative teachings, we uncover the technique known as "I Remember When." This method, grounded in the simplicity and potency of memory and emotion, offers a straightforward pathway to manifestation, specifically catering to those who seek an alternative to intensive visualization practices.

This technique stands out for its unique approach to leveraging past experiences as a means of shaping future realities. It begins with a critical examination of one's current emotional state, emphasizing the necessity of a positive and tranquil mindset as the foundation for successful manifestation. The method advocates for initiating the process from a place of emotional equilibrium, suggesting that a serene and content state of mind is the ideal setting for the seeds of desire to take root and flourish.

The next step involves pinpointing a singular, crystalline

desire. Unlike the broader approach of the "Isn't it Wonderful?" method, "I Remember When" channels its energy toward manifesting one specific aspiration at a time, concentrating efforts to magnify the likelihood of realization. The selected desire thus becomes the centerpiece of a series of reflective affirmations, each prefaced with "I remember when." These affirmations ingeniously navigate the journey from past challenges to present achievements, encapsulating the transformative essence of the technique.

For instance, envisioning financial prosperity might inspire reflections such as, "I remember when financial limitations hindered my experiences," or "I remember when owning my dream car felt like an unattainable fantasy." Each affirmation serves to acknowledge former trials while simultaneously heralding their resolution in the current reality. This subtle yet profound shift in perspective cultivates an environment ripe for gratitude and fulfillment, signaling to the subconscious that the aspired state has already been attained.

At the heart of the "I Remember When" technique lies its capacity to reframe past adversities as stepping stones to current successes. By positioning previous hardships as chapters that have been overcome, the method nurtures a sense of appreciation for the present, paving the way for desires to manifest with relative ease. It transforms memory into a dynamic force for manifestation, where each recollection contributes to the unfolding of one's desired state.

Neville Goddard's teachings provide a luminous guide on harnessing this technique to its fullest potential, illuminating the path to melding imagination with affirmative declarations. He inspires practitioners to not only envision external transformations but also to perceive themselves as the embodiment of their desires. Through this introspective journey, one can effectively "remember" their way into a renewed reality, where health, happiness, and prosperity reflect an inner state of achievement.

"You rise to a higher level of consciousness by taking your attention away from your present limitations and placing it upon that which you desire to be. Do not attempt this in day-dreaming or wishful thinking but in a positive manner. Claim yourself to be the thing desired. I AM that no sacrifice, no diet, no human tricks. All that is asked of you is to accept your desire. If you dare claim it, you will express it."

The "I Remember When" journey transcends mere reminiscence, evolving into an active re-envisioning of one's life story. It invites individuals to explore their past, not to linger on bygone struggles but to rejoice in their personal growth. This technique elucidates that remembering, when infused with deliberate intent and emotion, can emerge as a formidable instrument for crafting the future.

"Start now to remember when your friend wasn't well by imagining he is healthy. Remember when your daughter was single by imagining she is married. Go through life remembering when. Haven't you heard people say: 'Who

does he think he is? I remember when he had nothing and was a nobody!' Now, you may have heard a little jealousy in their tone and that is good because envy adds fire to the statement, which causes the one spoken of to have more! He may never know who caused his success, but it was done by an act of remembrance with intensity."

In its essence, the "I Remember When" technique is not merely a manifesting method; it is a testament to the fluidity of reality as experienced through the prism of personal perception. It offers a blueprint for traversing the realm of desires, guided by the luminaries of memory and imagination, toward the actualization of one's deepest aspirations. Through this practice, we discern that the past, present, and future are not isolated entities but interwoven strands in the tapestry of existence, meticulously crafted by the power of our thoughts and feelings.

MENTAL DIET

EMBARKING on the journey of manifestation with Neville Goddard's guidance illuminates the principle that the act of desiring initiates the process of bringing a wish into physical existence. Goddard's assertion that "creation is finished" underlines the omnipresence of every conceivable desire within the ether, awaiting our perception to align with its frequency for it to materialize in our reality. This notion challenges the conventional reliance on our physical senses to discern the boundaries of existence, urging us to transcend these limitations and embrace the vastness of consciousness itself.

The physical senses, though instrumental in navigating the tangible world, offer a restricted view of the universe's boundless nature. This limitation fosters a reality confined to what is immediately perceivable, obscuring the infinite possibilities that exist beyond sensory detection. Goddard invites us to reconsider our understanding of existence, suggesting that our desires, no matter how grand or elusive, are already woven into the fabric of reality, residing as potentialities within the quantum field. The task then becomes not one of creation but of selection—tuning into the desired frequency and embedding it within our subconscious to usher it into the physical realm.

Goddard's foundational manifestation method hinges on the practice of embodying the feeling of the fulfilled desire, a concept further emphasized through visualization and imaginal acts. This practice, however, is merely the beginning. True manifestation requires a steadfast commitment to the desired reality, extending beyond momentary visualizations to encompass our entire mental landscape. This involves not only the nurturing of positive imaginal acts but also the vigilant maintenance of our internal dialogue to support this new reality.

For instance, manifesting health transcends the visualization of wellness; it necessitates a conscious effort to redirect any negative internal conversations about illness or incapacity. Such contradictions between our imaginal acts and daily thought patterns dilute the potency of our manifestations, creating a tug-of-war within our consciousness that hinders progress. Goddard introduces the concept of a "mental diet" as a crucial adjunct to the manifestation process, emphasizing the need to curate our inner conversations as meticulously as we would our physical nourishment.

"Talking to oneself is a habit everyone indulges in. We could no more stop talking to ourselves than we could stop eating and drinking. All that we can do is control the nature and the direction of our inner conversations. Most of us are totally unaware of the fact that our inner conversations are the causes of the circumstances of our life."

A mental diet involves a vigilant awareness of our thoughts, particularly those that run counter to our desires. This practice calls for an alignment between our deepest aspirations and our moment-to-moment internal narratives, ensuring that our mental space supports rather than sabotages our goals. Whether it's wealth, love, or health we seek, the discipline of a mental diet teaches us to eschew thoughts of lack, unworthiness, or illness in favor of affirmations that resonate with our intended outcomes.

Goddard suggests practical methods to enhance self-awareness and control over our thoughts, including mindfulness meditation, nature walks, and journaling. These practices serve not just as tools for manifestation but as gateways to a more conscious and deliberate way of living, where we assume the role of architects of our reality.

The efficacy of a mental diet, much like its nutritional counterpart, hinges on consistency and perseverance. The journey is marked by inevitable missteps where negative thoughts encroach upon our mental space. Yet, it is our willingness to recalibrate and persist in our efforts that ultimately carves the path to manifestation.

One of Neville Goddard's shared success stories exemplifies the transformative power of a mental diet. A woman, struggling with her employer's unjust criticism, discovered that her internal grievances were manifesting as external conflicts. By changing her inner dialogue to one of gratitude and recognition, she witnessed a profound shift in her employer's attitude, reflecting the positivity she cultivated within. This narrative underscores the reciprocal nature of our internal and external worlds, illustrating how a change in our inner conversations can alter our life's circumstances.

As we navigate the complexities of reality creation, Goddard's teachings offer a beacon of clarity, reminding us that the realm of possibilities is boundless and inherently accessible. The key lies in attuning our consciousness to the frequency of our desires, supported by a disciplined mental diet that nurtures our aspirations into being. Through this holistic approach to manifestation, we unlock the potential to transform our lives, embodying the essence of our dreams in the tangible world.

.

SELF-CONCEPT

EMBRACING the profound insight of Neville Goddard's teachings brings us to the doorstep of a transformative practice known as "Self-Concept." This technique delves deep into the essence of how we perceive and value ourselves, underscoring the pivotal role our self-perception plays in shaping our life experiences. Through self-concept, we are invited to examine the mirror of our minds, reflecting on the person we see, our feelings towards our evolving journey, and our sense of worthiness concerning life's blessings.

Self-concept, as Goddard illuminates, is more than just an exercise in self-reflection; it is a powerful mechanism for manifesting the reality we desire. The way we habitually think and feel about ourselves sets the groundwork for the life we lead and the experiences we attract. It's a principle that reveals how individuals with a naturally strong and positive self-concept seem to effortlessly attract abundance, success, and fulfillment.

These individuals, blessed with either an inherited sense of self-worth or one cultivated through positive reinforcement, navigate life's challenges with an enviable ease. Their lives are testimonies to the magnetic power of a robust self-concept, drawing towards them opportunities and joy that many strive hard to achieve. Observing such people can be a source of inspiration, a reminder that the universe does indeed respond to our inner state of being.

For those who feel they lack this innate gift, Neville's teachings offer a beacon of hope. The realization that it's never too late to reshape our self-concept and, by extension, our destiny, is liberating. This journey begins with a thorough understanding of our current self-concept, built upon the beliefs we hold about ourselves and the thoughts that populate our minds daily.

Exploring these beliefs and thoughts requires introspection, often achieved through practices like meditation that allow us to peer into the depths of our subconscious. It's here, in the quietude of self-examination, that we can uncover the underlying beliefs that dictate our life patterns, especially in areas where we experience recurring challenges.

"It is our conception of ourselves which frees or constrains us, though it may use material agencies to achieve its purpose. Because life molds the outer world to reflect the inner arrangement of our minds, there is no way of bringing about the outer perfection we seek other

than by the transformation of ourselves. No help cometh from without; the hills to which we lift our eyes are those of an inner range. It is thus to our own consciousness that we must turn to the only reality, the only foundation on which all phenomena can be explained. We can rely absolutely on the justice of this law to give us only that which is of the nature of ourselves. To attempt to change the world before we change our concept of ourselves is to struggle against the nature of things."

This profound understanding emphasizes the necessity of shifting our focus inwards, toward a reevaluation and renewal of our self-concept. The transformation Goddard speaks of entails a conscious decision to detach from past versions of ourselves that no longer serve our highest good, actively curating a new identity that aligns with our deepest aspirations.

Journaling, mindfulness meditation, and immersing oneself in nature are proposed as methods to cultivate self-awareness and facilitate this transition. These practices enable us to sift through our mental chatter, identify disempowering beliefs, and replace them with empowering narratives that reflect our desired reality.

Embracing a new self-concept is akin to putting on a new pair of glasses through which the world is seen in a different light. The once seemingly insurmountable challenges transform into stepping stones leading us toward our goals. By consciously choosing the thoughts and beliefs that nurture our new identity, we open ourselves to the infinite possibilities that life has to offer.

In essence, self-concept is not just a technique; it's a journey of self-discovery and empowerment. Through the lens of this practice, we learn that our external circumstances are but reflections of our inner world. As we cultivate a self-concept rooted in love, worthiness, and abundance, we align ourselves with the universe's infinite generosity, ready to receive all the good it has in store.

Neville Goddard's insights into self-concept offer a roadmap to transforming our lives from the inside out. It's a reminder that the keys to the kingdom of our desires lie within the realms of our consciousness, waiting to be discovered and utilized. As we embark on this journey of self-reinvention, we are reminded that the only limits to what we can achieve and experience are those we impose upon ourselves. Through self-concept, we are empowered to dismantle these barriers, reconstructing our reality in the image of our highest aspirations.

TELEPHONE METHOD

YOUR JOURNEY with Neville Goddards teachings, while profound, can often feel like navigating through a fog—our senses, marvelous yet limited, can only perceive so much, leaving us yearning for some sign, some manifestation that our efforts are bearing fruit. It's in this space of uncertainty that the practice of making manifestation a joyous, lively process becomes invaluable.

Neville Goddard, a master of manifesting, understood the human inclination towards ennui and introduced various methods to invigorate the creative process. Among these, the telephone method stands out for its blend of simplicity and ingenuity, a technique that marries the ordinary act of conversation with the extraordinary power of focused imagination.

"I have found my telephone technique infallible. It never fails me. One day a friend called to tell me she wanted to

take an examination to become a court reporter. Giving me nine reasons why she could never pass the test, I changed every one as I heard it, and when the conversation was finished, I imagined an entirely different one. I heard her tell me she had passed the test with flying colors. My friend took the test, and although during the interval of six weeks she remained negative, I continued to believe she had passed.

Then one day she called, saying: 'Do you remember when I took the test?' and I replied: 'Yes, and you passed.' Then she said: 'Yes, but aren't you surprised?' I have been trying to tell her that imagining creates reality, but she cannot understand how an imaginal act unseen by the human senses can be held onto and produce results, but I know it always does!" Goddard shared. His friend's eventual success, despite her doubts, underscored the efficacy of this method, proving once again that "imagining creates reality."

The essence of the telephone method lies not in its mechanics but in the transformation it invites. It requires no special skills, just a willingness to engage one's imagination actively. Whether addressing a current problem or aiming for a desired outcome, the method shifts the participant from a passive state of wanting to an active state of creating.

Implementing this method could be as straightforward as having a phone conversation about a pressing issue while simultaneously imagining a resolution has already been joyfully reached. This dual action—speaking in the present while imagining a desired future—creates a dynamic mental environment where the desired outcome feels increasingly real.

Alternatively, the technique can be practiced solo, with the individual creating a vivid imaginal scene of receiving a phone call delivering the good news of their desire's fulfillment. The key here is detail: the sound of the ring, the voice on the other end, the surge of relief and joy at the resolution or achievement. Each element adds to the potency of the scene, embedding the desired outcome deeper into the fabric of one's reality.

Moreover, this method offers a delightful way to extend one's manifesting capabilities to benefit others. Imagining a friend sharing their success or joy over the phone not only aids them in their journey but reinforces the practitioner's belief in the power of their creative imagination.

For beginners or those seasoned in the art of manifesting, the telephone method proves that imagination needs no complex apparatus to be effective. A simple phone call, real or imagined, becomes a conduit for change, demonstrating that the tools for creating our reality are always at our disposal, as mundane as they may seem.

This technique also dovetails neatly with the principle of revision, another of Goddard's teachings, by refusing to accept any narrative that does not align with one's desired outcome. In doing so, it not only accelerates the manifestation process but enriches it, making the journey towards our desires not just a path to be walked but a dance to be enjoyed.

In sum, the telephone method illuminates the playful yet profound nature of manifesting. It teaches that joy, imagination, and a simple phone call can bridge the gap between desire and reality, reminding us that the universe is always listening, always ready to respond to our creative call.

LULLABY METHOD

EXPLORING NEVILLE GODDARD'S "LULLABY METHOD" reveals a pathway to manifestation that simplifies the creative process, making it accessible even to those who may struggle with visualization. This method, while echoing the principles of the State Akin to Sleep (SATS), distills the essence of desire into a potent emotional seed, fostering an environment where multiple or singular desires can flourish without the intricacies of detailed visualization.

Goddard's teachings underscore the transformative power of our self-concept and its pivotal role in shaping the tapestry of our lives. By aligning our internal narrative with our desires, we construct a reality that mirrors our most profound aspirations. The Lullaby Method embodies this principle, offering a streamlined approach to embedding our desires into the fabric of our consciousness.

"A most effective way to embody a desire is to assume the

**feeling of the wish fulfilled and then, in a relaxed and
sleepy state, repeat over and over again like a lullaby, any
short phrase which implies fulfillment of your desire,
such as, thank you, thank you, thank you, until the single
sensation of thankfulness dominates the mind."**
– Neville Goddard

This method begins with clarity—knowing precisely what you wish to manifest, be it a singular desire or a bouquet of aspirations. It encourages a shift in perspective, urging practitioners to view their lives through a spiritual lens, recognizing the seamless continuity of past, present, and future. In doing so, we are reminded of our innate power to mold our destiny through the simple yet profound act of assumption.

**"The natural man receiveth not the things of the spirit of
God for they are foolishness unto him; neither can he
know them for they are spiritually discerned."**
– Corinthians 2:14

Goddard differentiates between the natural view of life, bound by the limitations of current reality, and the spiritual view, which transcends time and circumstance. This spiritual perspective empowers us to enact change not just in our future but allows us to reinterpret our past, aligning our entire existence with our deepest desires.

The Lullaby Method is elegantly simple: in a state of relaxation, evoke the feeling of having already received your desire, then gently repeat a concise, affirming phrase—like a soothing lullaby—until it saturates your consciousness and lulls you into sleep. This repetition acts as a bridge, connecting your current state with the reality of your fulfilled wish, embedding the essence of your desire into the subconscious.

One remarkable success story illustrating the power of the Lullaby Method involves a woman who desired a new home. For months, she would drift off to sleep repeating, "Everything is done!", embodying the sensation of already residing in her dream home. Her unwavering focus on the feeling of fulfillment, rather than the minutiae of how her desire would materialize, paved the way for her wish to manifest. An unexpected financial gift from her father enabled her to secure her dream home, one that perfectly matched the vision she had nurtured through her nightly practice.

The Lullaby Method not only simplifies the manifestation process but also reinforces the principle that our reality is shaped by our dominant emotional states and assumptions. By adopting a phrase that resonates with the essence of our desire and repeating it with heartfelt emotion, we invite our dreams into our waking reality.

This method affirms that manifestation is not a laborious task but a gentle, joyous act of creation. It underscores the truth that within the quietude of our minds and hearts lies the power to transform our lives, proving, once again, that the imagination, cradled by emotion and faith, is the wellspring of all creation.

PRAYER

Manifestation, creating your own reality, and the wisdom of the new age may feel like concepts just within your grasp, recently brought into your awareness. Before encountering these transformative ideas, what was your recourse when faced with dilemmas beyond your earthly comprehension? For many, the answer lay in the ancient, universal act of prayer, a sacred communion seeking divine intervention and guidance.

Prayer transcends cultural and religious boundaries, offering solace and hope across generations and civilizations. It represents not just a call for divine assistance but a profound acknowledgment of a power greater than our mortal struggles, illuminating paths through the darkest valleys of human experience.

Neville Goddard, whose insights into the power of imagination and consciousness have enlightened many, also revered prayer, not as a mere ritual but as a potent force for manifesting desires.

"Therefore, I say to you, 'Whatever you ask for in prayer, have faith that you have received it, and it will be yours' (Mark 11, verse 24)".

In Goddard's view, prayer was not about petitioning an external deity but about realizing and activating the divine power within each individual. This perspective transforms prayer from a plea for external change to a conscious creation of desired realities.

For Goddard, the key to effective prayer lies in its approach. He teaches that the essence of prayer is not in the asking but in the feeling of having already received. This shift from wanting to having changes the nature of prayer from one of yearning to one of acceptance and gratitude.

Silence, Goddard argues, is foundational to this process. In the stillness of solitude, away from the distractions of the external world, one can truly connect with their inner divinity, their I AM-ness. This connection is crucial for realizing the power we hold to shape our realities.

"All of humanity's problems stem from man's inability to sit quietly in a room alone."
– Blaise Pascal

This quote echoes Goddard's sentiment that true change, true manifestation, begins within the quiet of our own hearts and minds. It's in this silence that we can reflect on our self-concept, our desires, and the infinite potential that lies within us to bring about the life we yearn for.

Connecting with the I AM-ness within us, we align with the creative force of the universe. Goddard emphasizes that prayer is a dialogue with this aspect of ourselves, a recognition of our divine essence capable of manifesting our deepest desires.

By affirming our desired state with the powerful declaration of I AM, we not only define our desires but also align our entire being with the reality of their fulfillment.

"You should awaken within you the feeling that you are and have that which heretofore you desired to be and possess. This is easily done by contemplating the joy that would be yours were your objective an accomplished fact so that you live and move and have your being in the feeling that your wish is realized."

Goddard's guidance encourages us to live as if our prayers have already been answered, embodying the fulfillment of our desires with every fiber of our being. This embodiment is the essence of successful prayer—a total and unshakeable faith in the realization of our wishes.

In a world often fixated on the external, Goddard's teachings remind us of the profound power of gratitude and faith. Successful prayer, he suggests, culminates in a simple yet profound act of thankfulness to the divine creativity within us.

"Take my message to heart and live by it. Practice the art of prayer daily, and then one day you will find the most effective prayer is: 'Thank you Father.' You will feel this being within you as your very self. If I want something, I know the desire comes from the Father, because all thought springs from Him. Having given me the urge, I thank Him for fulfilling it. Then I walk by faith, in confidence that he who gave it to me through the medium of desire will clothe it in bodily form for me to encounter in the flesh. Don't get in the habit of judging and criticizing, seeing only unlovely things.

You have a life – live it nobly. It is so much easier to be noble, generous, loving, and kind, than to be judgmental. If others want to do so, let them. They are an aspect of yourself that you haven't overcome yet, but don't fall into that habit. Simply thank your heavenly Father over and over and over again, because in the end, when the curtain comes down on this wonderful drama, the supreme actor will rise from it all and you will know that you are HE."
– Neville Goddard (The Secret of Prayer, 1967)

Through prayer, as Goddard teaches, we not only seek but also affirm and receive. We enter into a sacred partnership with the creative force of the universe, manifesting not just the fulfillment of personal desires but the realization of our divine essence.

EAVESDROPPING METHOD

THIS METHOD, standing out for its minimal reliance on visual imagery, is perfect for individuals seeking a more straightforward path to manifest their desires, particularly when those desires are numerous and varied. The core of this technique, like many of Goddard's teachings, revolves around the pivotal role of feelings in the manifestation process. Here, the focus is not just on generating any feeling but on capturing the essence of your desire's fulfillment with precision and depth.

Neville Goddard's teachings consistently underscore the idea that our external reality is a direct reflection of our inner state of consciousness. This inner state is a complex interplay of our emotions, beliefs, thoughts, and overall mood. In his work, Goddard emphasizes the transformative power of feelings, suggesting that they are the conduit through which our consciousness can alter our physical experiences. According to Goddard, to change one's life, it is essential first to shift one's state of consciousness. This notion is beautifully encapsulated in the principle that "feeling is the secret" to manifesting one's desires. Whether it's aspiring for wealth, health, or love, the key lies in aligning your feelings with the state of having already achieved these desires.

The eavesdropping technique is an innovative way to embody this principle. It involves mentally overhearing a conversation between two people close to you, discussing your successes in glowing terms. Imagine the warmth and confidence that would fill you upon hearing loved ones speak of your achievements with admiration and pride. This mental exercise not only affirms your success but also reinforces the interconnectedness and fluidity of our perceptions and reality, aligning perfectly with Goddard's assertion that "everyone is you pushed out."

Goddard's philosophy posits that we are all one, divinely interconnected. He elucidates this concept by highlighting our shared divine essence, suggesting that we are all playing various roles in a grand cosmic play, wearing masks that belie our true unified nature. This realization is pivotal in understanding the eavesdropping technique's effectiveness.

"May I tell you: it's the same story over and over again. You are the only Christ, the only Lord, the Only God, and Father of all! Having conceived the play, you are playing every part and each in his own wonderful time will play the part of Jesus Christ, for in the end we will all know that we are God. Then you will hate no one, for you will

realize that we agreed to play all the parts while hiding behind the masks we wear."

To utilize the eavesdropping method effectively, you start by clearly defining your desire. This specificity is crucial, as it sets the stage for the mental scenario you'll be creating. After achieving a relaxed state—ideal for this practice right before sleep—you engage in a mental simulation where you 'overhear' a conversation between two people who matter to you, discussing your achieved desire. The beauty of this technique lies in its simplicity and its reliance on auditory imagination, providing a refreshing alternative to visual-based manifestation methods.

This imaginative process is not just about hearing your successes being celebrated; it's about feeling the implications of those successes. It's about knowing, deep within your being, that you have achieved what you set out to do. The conversation you overhear should be imbued with details that make it as real and convincing as possible, from the tone of voice to the specific words of praise used. This mental enactment helps solidify the state of your wish fulfilled, marking a significant step towards its manifestation in your physical reality.

Goddard's teachings encourage a holistic integration of this imaginative act into your daily routine, emphasizing consistency and emotional investment. The eavesdropping method, while simple, is a potent tool in the manifestor's arsenal, offering a unique way to affirm one's desires and align oneself with the feeling of their fulfillment.

"If your income had just been increased to say $30,000 a year from your present income of less than $10,000, how would you feel? How would your present circle of friends see you? Would they know it? Would they discuss it? Would they speak of the change in your life? Tell them, and then eavesdrop and hear your friends discuss you as one who is now making $30,000 a year. That's a motion in God and that movement will produce results! Everything in this world is nothing more than the result of a movement in God, which is a motion in your wonderful imagination."

Through the eavesdropping technique, Goddard offers a pathway to manifestation that is grounded in the sensory experience of hearing, diversifying the ways in which we can align our internal state with our external desires. This method stands as a testament to the simplicity, effectiveness, and creative potential inherent in Goddard's approaches to manifestation, encouraging practitioners to explore the vast landscape of their

imagination to create the reality they desire. It underscores the importance of feelings in shaping our experiences and invites us to embrace the power of positive assumptions to transform our lives in profound ways.

SCRIPTING

SCRIPTING, as illuminated by Neville Goddard, serves as a dynamic bridge that connects conscious desires with the unconscious power of manifestation. It brings to life the essence of creation through the written word. Celebrated for its simplicity and potency, this technique allows individuals to meticulously craft their desired reality, imbuing each word with the vibrational essence of their dreams and aspirations.

To harness the full potential of scripting, one must integrate it as a practice that aligns with Neville Goddard's principle of embodying the state of the wish fulfilled. Here's how to use scripting to manifest your desires effectively:

1. **Set Your Intention:** Clearly define what you wish to manifest. Whether it's a personal transformation, artistic achievement, fulfilling relationships, or improved health, your intention should be precise.

2. **Embody the Wish Fulfilled:** Write from the perspective of already having achieved your goal. This means scripting your life as if your desires are currently your reality, capturing the emotions and experiences associated with this fulfillment.

3. **Detail Your Script:** Describe your envisioned reality with vivid details. Include sensory descriptions, emotional responses, and actions that resonate with achieving your goal. The depth of your description amplifies the manifestation power of your script.

4. **Maintain Regular Engagement:** Make scripting a daily or weekly habit. Consistency reinforces your intentions and strengthens your alignment with your desires.

5. **Release and Trust:** Once you've scripted your desires, let go of any attachment to the outcomes. Have faith in the universe to bring your desires to fruition in the most beneficial manner.

6. **Reflect and Adjust:** Periodically review your scripts to see if they still resonate with your desires. As you grow and evolve, your aspirations might change. Update your scripts accordingly to reflect your current state of desire and understanding.

Consider aiming to deepen your artistic connection. Through scripting, envision yourself fully immersed in your creative process, detailing mornings spent in your studio where inspiration flows freely. Imagine the joy of sharing your work, receiving positive feedback, and feeling deeply connected to your artistic path. This visualization isn't just fantasy; it aligns your energy with the universe, paving the way for these experiences to manifest.

In the realm of personal growth, scripting can be a transformative tool. Envision overcoming personal barriers, engaging in enriching conversations, and establishing healthier relationships. By scripting these scenarios, you're not only preparing for real-life challenges but also reshaping your self-perception to embody resilience and confidence.

For those facing health challenges, scripting serves as a means to visualize and enact the journey from illness to wellness. Write about waking up feeling rejuvenated, partaking in activities you love, and celebrating health milestones. This practice shifts your focus from limitations to possibilities, aiding your mind and body in the healing process.

In seeking deeper, meaningful relationships, script scenarios of harmonious interactions, understanding, and love. Visualize the development of a romantic relationship founded on mutual respect and shared dreams. Scripting in this manner actively shapes your emotional landscape, attracting and nurturing the bonds you desire.

Scripting is more than a manifestation technique; it's a profound act of co-creation with the universe. Each script is a declaration of intent, a meticulously crafted blueprint for the reality you wish to create. By engaging in scripting with belief and dedication, you can alter the course of your life, turning the pages of your journal into stepping stones toward realizing your deepest desires and aspirations.

Scripting is not merely about writing a story; it's about authoring your destiny, one word at a time, guided by the infinite wisdom and power encapsulated in Neville Goddard's teachings.

PART IV
MASTERING THE ART OF MANIFESTATION

THE SHOCKING MANIFESTATION MISTAKES YOU DIDN'T KNOW YOU WERE MAKING!

IN THE STUDY of Neville Goddard's teachings on manifestation, it becomes clear that the path is full of potential obstacles that must be navigated carefully to achieve the desired result. This journey, while promising the realization of one's deepest desires, demands more than mere wishful thinking—it calls for a profound internal shift, a transformation that aligns one's inner world with the external manifestation of their dreams. As we delve into the common errors that hinder the manifestation process, it is crucial to reflect upon Neville's teachings, which serve as beacons guiding us back to the true essence of creation.

One of the first missteps many encounter is the search for a quick fix, a shortcut to manifesting their desires without fully committing to the process. This approach, fueled by a culture of instant gratification, undermines the foundational principle of manifestation—that it is a journey of self-discovery and transformation. Neville Goddard's wisdom offers a counterpoint to this mindset, emphasizing the importance of patience and persistence. In his words:

"The world is yourself pushed out. Ask yourself what you want and then give it to yourself! Do not question how it will come about; just go your way knowing that the evidence of what you have done must appear, and it will."

This quote underscores the necessity of faith in the manifestation process, reminding us that the fulfillment of our desires is not a matter of if, but when.

Another critical mistake is failing to engage in self-reflection and personal development. Manifestation is not merely about visualizing an outcome but about becoming a vessel through which that outcome can materialize. This transformation requires an intimate understanding of one's self, an alignment of thought, emotion, and belief that resonates with the desired state. Neville eloquently captures this concept, stating:

"You must be in the state of the wish fulfilled until you feel the thrill of Victory. Then, with confidence born of the knowledge of this law, watch the physical realization of your objective."

This emphasizes the integral role of self-belief and the cultivation of an inner state that mirrors the outer desire.

A pervasive error in the practice of manifestation is underestimating the power of one's divine essence, the "I AM-ness" that Neville frequently references. This divine aspect of our being is the true source of our creative power, yet many of us fail to fully embrace this potential. Neville Goddard elucidates this point, asserting:

"Be still and know that you are that which you desire to be, and you will never have to search for it."

Here, Neville highlights the necessity of acknowledging and embodying our divine nature, recognizing ourselves as the architects of our reality.

The tendency to cling to the past, to allow past experiences and traumas to define our present and future, is another stumbling block on the path to manifestation. Neville advocates for a conscious detachment from the past, urging us to embrace a new narrative that aligns with our aspirations. He advises:

"Disregard appearances, conditions, in fact all evidence of your senses that deny the fulfillment of your desire. Rest in the assumption that you are already what you want to be, for in that determined assumption you and your infinite Being are merged in creative unity, and with your infinite Being (God) all things are possible."

This counsel encourages us to sever ties with the past and to dwell in the reality of our wishes fulfilled.

Lastly, the attempt to control every aspect of the manifestation process reflects a misunderstanding of the principles at play. True manifestation requires a surrender to the wisdom of our higher self, a trust in the natural unfolding of our desires. Neville captures this sentiment, reminding us:

"You do not command things to appear by your words or loud affirmations. Such vain repetition is more often than not confirmation of the opposite. Decreeing is ever done in consciousness. That is, every man is conscious of being that which he has decreed himself to be."

In addressing these manifestation errors with the guidance of Neville Goddard's teachings, we pave the way for a more authentic and powerful journey towards realizing our desires. Through patience, self-awareness, acknowledgment of our divine essence, release from the past, and surrender to the greater wisdom within, we align ourselves with the universal law of creation. These principles, when truly embodied, open the doors to a life where every dream is not just a possibility but an inevitable reality.

CRACK THE MANIFESTATION CODE: UNVEILING THE TRAITS OF SUCCESS

❦

UNDERSTANDING the subtle nuances and traits that distinguish successful manifesters from those still on their path to discovery can be transformative. Its not just about uncovering "secrets" but about integrating profound truths into one's life, thereby transitioning from the vast majority into the realm of true creators.

Curiosity and a Commitment to Learning: The hallmark of successful manifesters is their insatiable curiosity and commitment to continuous learning. They approach the art of manifestation with an open heart and mind, eager to explore and understand the depths of their own consciousness and the laws that govern reality. This relentless pursuit of knowledge is not a chore but a journey of discovery, where each step brings them closer to their true potential. They understand that the process of manifestation is a profound subject that requires dedication, experimentation, and patience. Successful manifesters know that there is no one-size-fits-all approach. Instead, they explore various techniques and teachings, including those of Neville Goddard, to find what resonates most deeply with their unique circumstances and aspirations.

Personal Responsibility and Trust in the Process: Another distinguishing trait is the deep sense of personal responsibility that successful manifesters carry. They recognize that the power to change their reality lies within them and that external circumstances are but reflections of their internal state. This understanding compels them to take full ownership of their thoughts, emotions, and actions, knowing that these are the building blocks of their reality. They are inspired by stories like Neville's encounter with Abdullah, where the emphasis on personal responsibility and trust in the process are pivotal. Successful manifesters do not seek quick fixes or external validation but rather focus on aligning their inner world with the reality they wish to create, fully trusting that the universe will conspire in their favor.

Unwavering Positive Expectations: The ability to maintain positive expectations, even in the face of adversity, is a critical aspect of successful manifestation. These individuals have cultivated a mindset that expects the best outcomes, thereby attracting positive circumstances and opportunities into their lives. They embody the teachings of Neville Goddard, who emphasized the power of assumptions and the role of consciousness in shaping reality. By expecting good things to happen, successful manifesters create a fertile ground for their desires to manifest.

Resilience Against Doubt: A key characteristic that sets successful manifesters apart is their resilience against doubt. Doubt can be a significant barrier to manifestation, as it undermines the belief and confidence required to bring one's desires into reality. Successful manifesters have mastered the art of maintaining a strong belief in their vision, despite external circumstances or temporary setbacks. They understand that doubt is a natural part of the human experience but refuse to let it dictate their journey. Instead, they focus on reinforcing their faith and belief in the inevitable manifestation of their desires.

The Power of Scripting: Successful manifesters also understand and utilize the power of scripting. This technique involves writing down one's desires and future realities in a detailed and present-tense format, thereby bringing them into the now. Scripting allows for a deep immersion in the desired state, making it easier to embody the feelings associated with the wish fulfilled. Through scripting, manifesters create a bridge between their current reality and the one they aspire to, reinforcing their intentions and accelerating the manifestation process.

In conclusion, successful manifesters are distinguished by their curiosity, commitment to learning, personal responsibility, positive expectations, resilience against doubt, and the strategic use of techniques like scripting. These traits, deeply rooted in the teachings of Neville Goddard, serve as a blueprint for anyone seeking to transform their dreams into reality. By embodying these characteristics, one embarks on a transformative journey of self-discovery and creation, unlocking the full potential of their manifesting abilities.

PART V

THE 5 STEP PROTOCOL FOR MANIFESTING ANYTHING

THE CLARITY EXERCISE

"If A Man Knows Not To Which Port He Sails, No Wind Is Favorable."
– Seneca

Embarking on the journey of manifestation with Neville Goddard's teachings as our guide, we're reminded by Seneca's timeless insight, "If a Man Knows Not to Which Port He Sails, No Wind Is Favorable." This adage under-scores the necessity of having a clear destination in mind before setting sail on the vast sea of possibilities. Without a defined goal, the journey of manifestation can become aimless, lacking the direction needed to harness the winds of the universe favorably.

THE FIRST STEP: CLARITY OF DESIRE

Understanding precisely what you desire and the reasons behind these desires is the initial, critical step in the manifestation process. This clarity is not just about knowing what you want on a superficial level but under- standing the deep-seated 'why' behind each desire. In a world inundated with endless choices and bombarded by social media's portrayals of success and happiness, distin- guishing between fleeting whims and genuine, soul-stirring desires becomes essential.

Jim Rohn's concept of having a "list of why's" serves as a powerful tool in this discernment process. It compels us to examine our motivations and ensures that our efforts are directed towards truly meaningful objectives. The allure of social media trends and external influences can easily sway us, but true fulfillment comes from pursuing desires that resonate with our deepest selves.

THE CLARITY EXERCISE: IDENTIFYING YOUR TRUE DESIRES

To aid in achieving this clarity, a structured exercise is proposed. This involves categorizing your life into areas such as health, career, finances, relationships, and personal experiences, then deeply reflecting on what you wish to improve or achieve in each domain. This exercise is not merely an act of listing desires but a profound exploration of what genuinely matters to you.

- **Health:** Detail your current health challenges and envisage your ideal state of wellness.
- **Career:** Define your career aspirations for the short and long term.
- **Money:** Reflect on what financial success means to you and how it contributes to your life.
- **Relationships:** Consider the current state of your relationships and how you'd like them to evolve.
- **Experiences:** Identify the experiences that would add depth and joy to your life.

This clarity exercise goes beyond mere goal-setting; it's an introspective journey to uncover your heart's true desires.

EMBODYING THE MANIFESTATION MINDSET

With clarity about what you wish to manifest, the next steps involve embracing the mindset and habits of successful manifesters. This includes a relentless curiosity, a commitment to personal responsibility, and an unwavering belief in one's power to create reality.

Neville Goddard's teachings emphasize the significance of the "I AM-ness," the divine power within each individual to manifest their desires. He asserts, "I AM wealthy, poor, healthy, sick, free, confined were first of all impressions or conditions felt before they became visible expressions. Your world is your consciousness objectified."

Successful manifestation, therefore, hinges on aligning your inner state—your beliefs, thoughts, and feelings—with your desired outcomes. This alignment transforms the abstract into the tangible, turning dreams into lived experiences.

LAYING THE FOUNDATION FOR MANIFESTATION

The journey of manifestation begins with a clear vision of what you desire and why. Through the clarity exercise, you not only pinpoint your goals but also align your inner world to the reality you wish to create. As you embark on this journey, remember that manifestation is not a mere technique but a way of life, requiring dedication, self-awareness, and a deep belief in your power to shape your destiny.

As you move forward, armed with clarity and determination, the teachings of Neville Goddard and the wisdom of the ages serve as your compass, guiding you towards the fulfillment of your deepest desires.

ELEVATE YOUR SELF-CONCEPT

BEFORE DIVING into the depths of manifestation and unraveling the intricacies of Neville Goddard's teachings, it's crucial to ensure you've laid the groundwork with the clarity exercise from the previous segment. Manifestation isn't a race to the finish line but a step-by-step journey that builds upon each previous step. Rushing ahead without fully embracing and applying the initial steps is like trying to construct a building without a solid foundation—it simply won't stand.

The essence of manifestation lies in belief—not just a superficial nod to the idea that you can create your reality, but a deep, unshakable conviction in your own creative power. This belief transcends mere optimism; it's an understanding that life, in all its complexity and beauty, is a reflection of your consciousness. Your perception of yourself and the world around you shapes your reality more than any external factor ever could.

Life is akin to a mental game where the playing field is your consciousness, and the pieces are your beliefs, emotions, and thoughts. If you perceive yourself as a victim, the universe aligns with this belief, manifesting more situations that reinforce this perception. It's a self-fulfilling prophecy. However, when you begin to view yourself as the powerful creator you truly are, the game changes. The universe conspires to reflect this new self-concept, bringing opportunities and successes into your life.

The journey to manifesting your desires is essentially a journey back to your true self, to the realization that you are an extension of the divine energy that creates worlds. This isn't about adopting a new belief system but about remembering your inherent nature. When you understand that you're woven from the same fabric as the stars and galaxies, that the same force that breathes life into the universe breathes life into you, you unlock an infinite power to create.

Neville Goddard, through his teachings, invites us to reclaim this forgotten wisdom. He encourages us to adopt a mental diet that aligns with our aspirations, to cultivate thoughts that support our desires, and to steadfastly refuse to entertain doubts or fears. As Emmet Fox, another spiritual luminary, eloquently puts it:

"All day long the thoughts that occupy your mind, your Secret Place, as Jesus calls it, are molding your destiny for good or evil; in fact, the truth is that the whole of our life's experience is but the outer expression of inner

thought. Now we can choose the sort of thoughts that we entertain. It will be a little difficult to break a bad habit of thought, but it can be done. We can choose how we shall think—in point of fact, we always do choose—and therefore our lives are just the result of the kind of thoughts we have!"

In addition to careful monitoring of your thoughts, visualization and affirmations serve as powerful tools for embodying the person you wish to become. By regularly visualizing your ideal self and affirming your worth and capabilities, you begin to rewire your subconscious mind. This process of mental rehearsal gradually shifts your self-concept, aligning it with the reality you desire to manifest.

Listening to positive affirmations and engaging in visualization exercises not only boost your self-concept but also attune your vibration to the frequency of your desires. This alignment between your internal state and your external aspirations is the key to unlocking the doors to all you wish to manifest.

As you embark on this transformative journey, remember that manifestation is not a destination but a continuous process of aligning your inner world with the outer reality you seek to create. By building a strong foundation of self-belief, understanding the power of your consciousness, and utilizing the tools of mental diet, visualization, and affirmations, you step into your power as a conscious creator, capable of manifesting the life of your dreams.

SATURATE THE MIND WITH WISH FULFILLED

To MANIFEST your desires into tangible reality, it's imperative to immerse your consciousness fully in the state of your wish fulfilled, as masterfully taught by Neville Goddard. He imparts a timeless wisdom crucial for anyone looking to transform their life through the power of imagination:

"Assume the feeling of your wish fulfilled and continue feeling that it is fulfilled until that which you feel objictifies itself."

This principle lies at the core of manifesting your desires. It's about embodying the reality of your wishes so profoundly that your entire being—thoughts, actions, and emotions—aligns with the existence of your fulfilled desires. Essentially, living in the end or adopting the state of the wish fulfilled isn't mere daydreaming; it's an active, dynamic state where your life is in harmony with your desires, making them inevitable in your reality.

Neville further elucidates this concept, stressing the importance of your assumptions in shaping your life:

"The drama of life is a psychological one, and the whole of it is written and produced by your assumptions. Learn the art of assumption, for only in this way can you create your own happiness."

The essence of manifesting lies in the power of your imagination and its ability to convince your subconscious of the reality of your desires. The mind, incapable of distinguishing between vivid imagination and actual events, responds to your vividly imagined scenarios as if they were real, thereby setting the stage for their physical manifestation.

To fully embrace the state of the wish fulfilled, introspection is key. You must clearly differentiate between the feeling of having your desires and not having them. It's essential to familiarize yourself with the emotional and psychological landscape of your desired reality, breaking it down to the finest details, ensuring your mind is saturated with the feeling of having what you desire.

The practice of the State Akin to Sleep (SATS) is invaluable in this process. It serves as a direct conduit to your subconscious, allowing you to plant the seeds of your desires in the most receptive state of your mind. By engaging in SATS, you immerse yourself in a liminal space where the subconscious is most open to the impressions of your desires.

Neville's personal story of using the SATS method to manifest an honorable discharge from the army exemplifies the effectiveness of this technique. Despite his initial application being disapproved, Neville didn't waver in his belief. Instead, he employed SATS, vividly imagining himself honorably discharged and back at home. Night after night, he persisted in this imaginal act until his external reality conformed to his internal state:

"The soldier realized that his consciousness was the only reality, that his particular state of consciousness determined the events he would encounter. That night, in the interval between getting into bed and falling asleep, he concentrated on consciously using the law of assumption. In imagination, he felt himself to be in his own apartment in New York City.

He visualized his apartment, that is, in his mind's eye he actually saw his own apartment, mentally picturing each one of the familiar rooms with all the furnishings vividly real.

With this picture clearly visualized, and lying flat on his back, he completely relaxed physically. In this way, he induced a state bordering on sleep, at the same time retaining control of the direction of his attention. When his body was completely immobilized, he assumed that he was in his own room and felt himself to be lying in his own bed – a very different feeling from that of lying on an army cot.

In imagination, he rose from the bed, walked from room to room, touching various pieces of furniture. He then went to the window and, with his hands resting on the sill, looked out on the street on which his apartment faced. So vivid was all this in his imagination that he saw in detail the pave-ment, the railings, the trees and the familiar red brick of the building on the opposite side of the street. He then returned to his bed and felt himself drifting off to sleep.

He knew that it was most important in the successful use of this law that at the actual point of falling asleep, his consciousness was filled with the assumption that he was already what he wanted to be. All that he did in imagination was based on the assumption that he was no longer in the army. Night after night, the soldier enacted this drama. Night after night, in imagination, he felt himself, honorably discharged, back in his home, seeing all the familiar surroundings and falling asleep in his own bed. This continued for eight nights.

And on the ninth day, Neville finally got what he wanted. His application was honorably approved by the colonel.

When trying to saturate your mind with your desire, this is how you must utilize SATS too. Add all the sensory details of your desired reality, and then sleep in that

state. Night after night, just like Neville did. And then, the universe will ensure you get exactly what you intended to have."

This story is a testament to the transformative power of assumption and the practice of SATS. It illustrates how, by faithfully adopting the state of the wish fulfilled, you can alter your reality to reflect your deepest desires. Through disciplined imagination, embodying the feelings of your desires as already manifested, and persistently living in that state, you unlock the potential to manifest anything you desire.

Treading this journey of manifestation requires more than mere desire; it demands a profound belief in your creative power and the relentless pursuit of your state of wish fulfilled. As you navigate this path, let the principles taught by Neville Goddard illuminate your way, guiding you toward the realization of your dreams and the ultimate creation of your desired reality.

IGNORE THE 3D

❦

"If you are dissatisfied with your present expression in life, the only way to change it is to take your attention away from that which seems so real to you and rise in consciousness to that which you desire to be. You cannot serve two masters, therefore to take your attention from one state of consciousness and place it upon another is to die to one and live to the other."
– Neville Goddard

Navigating the gap between desire and its manifestation can be a journey fraught with patience and perseverance. Instant manifestations, while not unheard of, are rare, and the journey towards realizing your dreams often stretches across time. This interval, whether it spans days, months, or longer, can sometimes be a trial of faith and belief. But it's crucial to recognize that the duration your desires take to manifest is, in many ways, determined by you.

One of the fundamental reasons immediate manifestations are exceptional is the lack of a robust belief system. For your innermost desires to materialize in the physical world, your belief in their possibility must be unwavering. Yet, our past experiences often haunt our present attempts to create anew. The mind, a logical machine, calculates our past successes and failures, casting a shadow of doubt over our future endeavors. This retrospective analysis can erode the very foundation of hope needed to birth new realities.

Venturing into the past is akin to walking on quicksand. It's a place where old emotions and failures lurk, ready to pull you back. If you wish to forge a different life path, one that diverges from the narrative of your past, it's imperative to break free from its grasp. The inability to detach from past experiences is a significant barrier to the swift realization of your desires.

Moreover, the speed at which your desires manifest is also influenced by the mental barriers you've erected around them. Consider the ease with which you might manifest a vacant parking spot—a desire unburdened by doubt or perceived difficulty. Contrast this with the daunting task of winning a lottery, where mental resistance and ingrained beliefs about the improbability of such an event create a formidable blockade.

The law of assumption operates flawlessly in both scenarios, delivering precisely what you believe is within your reach. Thus, if your manifestation journey seems protracted, the manner in which you navigate this interim period becomes critically important.

Facing the 3D world, or your current reality, can often be disheartening. It serves as a constant reminder of what you've yet to achieve. However, it's vital to recognize that the 3D world is merely a reflection of past states of consciousness. It does not dictate your future. Maintaining your focus on your desired state, despite the contradictory evidence presented by your current circumstances, is key.

For instance, let's explore the scenario of manifesting a job promotion. You've done the work; you've envisioned your success and occupied the state of the wish fulfilled through nightly SATS practice. Yet, external circumstances at work—perhaps a colleague being favored for the position —challenge your belief in your desired outcome.

This is the moment to steadfastly redirect your focus back to your desire, irrespective of the external noise. You must choose, time and again, to align with your desired future rather than being swayed by present circumstances. This choice—to steadfastly believe in the reality of your wish fulfilled, even when everything around you suggests otherwise—is the crux of manifesting.

"The drama of life is a psychological one, and the whole of it is written and produced by your assumptions. Learn the art of assumption, for only in this way can you create your own happiness."
– Neville Goddard highlights the transformative power of our assumptions.

By consciously choosing to ignore the transient nature of 3D realities and remaining unwavering in your belief, you align yourself with the fundamental principles of manifestation. In this act of faith, where you refuse to acknowledge anything but the realization of your desires, lies the key to unlocking the life you yearn for.

THE MAGNIFICENT SURRENDER

REACHING the finale of our journey through the 5-step protocol for manifestation, we encounter the pivotal, yet often the most challenging step: the art of surrender. This step, the magnificent surrender, encapsulates the essence of releasing control and entrusting your desires to a force beyond your conscious efforts—the divine, the universe, your higher self.

Surrender, in the realm of manifestation, doesn't mean giving up on your dreams. Instead, it symbolizes a transition from active creation to a state of trust and belief in the process set in motion. It is an acknowledgment that while your desires are clear and your intentions set, the realization of these desires transcends your direct control.

Yet, the act of surrendering is counterintuitive to our innate desire to 'make things happen.' Throughout the manifestation process, from clarifying intentions to embodying the state of the wish fulfilled, there's a sense of active participation. This engagement feeds our belief in progress, providing a semblance of control over the outcome.

However, surrender calls for a cessation of this active engagement, introducing a period of seemingly paradoxical inaction. Herein lies the challenge: embracing the concept that achievements can unfold without relentless striving. This notion is at odds with the conventional programming of action leading to results, thus making surrender a daunting prospect for many.

The difficulty of surrender is magnified in an era dominated by instant gratification. The pervasive culture of immediate results, where desires are fulfilled at the click of a button, ill-prepares us for the patience required in the manifestation process. This impatience, a breeding ground for desperation and lack, starkly contrasts the mindset conducive to attracting desires.

In moments of impatience or when the desire lingers unmanifested, detachment becomes a powerful tool. By momentarily stepping back and diverting your focus to other pursuits or interests, you alleviate the pressure of the immediate realization of your desire. This detachment, far from apathy, is a strategic pause, allowing your desire the space to manifest free from the constraints of your urgent expectations.

A cornerstone of surrender is relinquishing the need to

decipher the 'how' of your desire's manifestation. The intricacies of its realization are beyond the purview of your conscious mind, entrusted instead to the universe's infinitely wise orchestration. This relinquishment of control is not a resignation but a profound act of faith in the universal order.

Dr. Joe Dispenza encapsulates this beautifully:

"Surrender deeper into intelligent love; Trust in the unknown; Continuously surrender some aspect of the limited self to join the greater self; Lose yourself in nothing to become everything; Relax into an infinite deep sea of coherent energy."

Embracing surrender is to embrace trust in a process that operates beyond the visible, measurable outcomes. It's an invitation to enjoy the richness of life in the interim, assured that what you seek is aligning with your reality in ways unfathomable to the logical mind.

The journey to understanding and truly living the principle of magnificent surrender may require time and practice. Yet, once experienced, the peace and assurance it brings to the manifestation process are transformative. It becomes less about the anxiety of waiting and more about the certainty of becoming, a transition from controlling to allowing, from doing to being.

In this surrender lies the ultimate freedom—the freedom to desire without desperation, to believe without seeing, and to receive with grace and gratitude. This step, though last in our protocol, is the beginning of a new relationship with the universe, where every desire set forth is met with a serene confidence in its unfolding.

PART VI

THE MONEY MANIFESTATION BLUEPRINT

START WITH GRATITUDE

WELCOME to the money manifestation blueprint, where you will learn the art of attracting money with simple methods and mental hacks. If applied correctly, the valuable information contained within the next three sections will put you ahead of the 95%. You will leave the ordinary and become the extraordinary. You will be set up for success like you have never been.

The Money Manifestation Blueprint blends spirituality and materialism to help you manifest financial abundance with the power of your consciousness. This blueprint, distilled from Neville Goddard's profound teachings and supplemented with practical techniques, is your gateway to transforming your financial reality.

Neville Goddard's assertion, **"CREATION IS ALREADY FINISHED!"**, serves as the foundational principle of this blueprint. Your desires, including the wealth you seek, already exist in the infinite realm of possibilities. The journey, then, is not about creating afresh but aligning yourself with the reality where your financial abundance is a lived truth.

The cornerstone of this alignment is gratitude. Gratitude transcends mere politeness; it is a potent vibrational state that aligns you with the frequency of abundance. It opens your being to receive, transforming your consciousness to one of wealth and prosperity. The practice of gratitude, therefore, is not just a preliminary step; it's a continual, integral part of the manifestation process.

Gratitude's transformative power lies in its dual ability to center your mind and shift your focus from lack to abundance. In the chaos and stress of daily life, gratitude is the beacon that guides you back to peace and creativity, the fertile ground where seeds of intention grow. It reassures the mind, easing it into a state where creation is not just possible but natural.

By focusing on the abundance already present in your life, gratitude amplifies your awareness of the universe's infinite resources. This realization is pivotal: it dismantles the scarcity mindset, revealing the truth of limitless abundance. The universe, abundant and ever-giving, assures that there's more than enough for everyone, debunking the myth of finite resources.

"Gratitude turns what we have into enough, and more. It turns denial into acceptance, chaos into order, confusion

into clarity...it makes sense of our past, brings peace for today, and creates a vision for tomorrow."
– Melody Beattie

This quote encapsulates the essence of gratitude's power. It is the alchemy that transforms your perspective, inviting order and clarity into your life. By acknowledging and appreciating what you have, you open the doors to more — more wealth, more joy, more of whatever you desire.

As you embark on this blueprint to financial abundance, let gratitude be your guide. Let it infuse your consciousness with a sense of peace, abundance, and receptivity. The Money Manifestation Blueprint is not just a series of steps; it's a transformational journey that begins with gratitude and culminates in the realization of your deepest desires for wealth and prosperity. Embrace this journey with an open heart, and watch as the universe aligns to bring your financial aspirations into reality.

VISUALIZE YOUR ABUNDANT FUTURE!

❧

IN ONE OF HIS LECTURES, Neville shares the story of his elder brother and how, through his imagination and persistence, he altered his financial conditions forever. His journey from financial struggle to prosperity exemplifies the transformative power of unwavering imagination and belief. Victor's story is not just a tale of achieving wealth; it's a testament to the principle that within the realm of imagination lies the seed of every possibility.

Victor found himself in a daunting financial predicament at the young age of twenty, with no foreseeable path to affluence. Yet, it was within this period of apparent scarcity that Victor chose to envision a future replete with abundance and success. His dream was specific: to own a large building and establish the Goddard family business within its premises. This dream, although grandiose to an outsider given Victor's financial state, was the canvas upon which Victor painted his future.

Each day, with disciplined regularity, Victor visited the very building he aspired to own, situating himself in front of it, allowing his imagination to envelop him in the reality of his desire. He envisioned "Goddard & Sons" emblazoned across the building, transforming the edifice from an external structure into a personal dream. His visualization wasn't a fleeting engagement; it was a ritual, performed with the same conviction and consistency for two years.

The universe, in its mysterious ways, orchestrated events in favor of Victor's vision. A stranger stepped forward, purchasing the building for the Goddard family under the condition of repayment over a decade. This seemingly miraculous development marked the inception of the Goddard family's ascent in the business world, all stemming from Victor's unwavering persistence and belief in his dream.

Victor's journey underscores a critical aspect of manifestation: the power of persistence in one's vision, coupled with an unshakeable belief in its realization. His story invites us to reflect on our desires and the depth of our commitment to them. Do we possess a vision that compels us to imagine against all odds? Are we prepared to nurture our dreams with the tenacity that Victor exemplified?

To harness the power of imagination in manifesting wealth, one effective strategy is visualization, particularly at the cusp of sleep when the mind is most receptive. Neville Goddard emphasizes this practice as a communion with the divine, a moment of unity with infinite intelligence. In this tranquil state, envision your life enriched with abundance, detailing the future where your financial aspirations are fulfilled. Allow these visualizations to permeate your consciousness nightly, solidifying them as your new reality.

Persist in this practice, drawing inspiration from Victor Goddard's story. Your financial goals, no matter how ambitious, are within the realm of possibility. Imbue your imagination with the richness of your desires and steadfastly maintain this vision, irrespective of external circumstances.

In the ensuing narrative of our Money Manifestation Blueprint, we will delve deeper into enhancing this foundational practice with additional strategies. These insights aim to elevate your manifestation journey, equipping you with the tools to transform your financial dreams into tangible reality.

As we proceed, remember the essence of Victor's story: the confluence of imagination, belief, and persistence is the crucible in which the extraordinary is forged. Embrace this triad as your guide, and step into the abundance that awaits.

COMBINE INSPIRED ACTION
WITH THE FLOW STATE

EMBARKING on the final leg of our journey into the realms of manifesting wealth, it becomes imperative to grasp the notion of taking inspired action and embracing the state of flow. This culmination of efforts not only solidifies your intentions in the physical world but also aligns you with the natural law of abundance, propelling you towards unparalleled financial success.

Inspired action, as opposed to mere activity, emerges from a place of passion and enthusiasm. It's an action taken with joy, where every step feels like a dance rather than a dreary march. When you engage in work that ignites your soul, the universe conspires to assist you, turning mundane tasks into stepping stones towards your grand financial aspirations.

Consider the concept of the flow state, eloquently described by Mihaly Csikszentmihalyi, which encapsulates the essence of being utterly absorbed in an activity. This state, where time seems to stand still and your skills are used to their utmost capacity, is where true genius unfolds. In this domain of peak performance, inspired action becomes not just a method, but a way of being, offering a direct conduit to achieving your financial goals with grace and ease.

"A state in which people are so involved in an activity that nothing else seems to matter; the experience is so enjoyable that people will continue to do it even at great cost, for the sheer sake of doing it."
– *Mihaly Csikszentmihalyi*

To navigate towards this state, begin by attuning to your emotional landscape. A balanced and serene mind is the fertile ground from which inspired actions sprout. By ensuring your work challenges and stimulates you, maintaining a balance between skill and task difficulty, you edge closer to the flow state, making each task a joyful expedition towards your goal.

Embracing positive affirmations can significantly bolster your journey. Asserting your autonomy and capability fortifies your belief in your power to shape your financial destiny. These affirmations, much like a mantra, reinforce your resolve and heighten your alignment with the abundance you seek.

As we conclude this blueprint, it's crucial to reflect on the essence of what you've learned. Manifesting wealth transcends mere desire; it's a symphony of imagination, belief, inspired action, and surrender. Each element plays a crucial role in crafting the life of prosperity you yearn for.

The journey of financial manifestation is a testament to your power as a creator. By aligning your intentions with inspired action and flow, you not only set the stage for abundance but also transform your relationship with wealth. This transformation is not just about acquiring riches but about becoming a person for whom abundance is a natural state of being.

As you venture forward, armed with the knowledge and techniques gleaned from this book, remember that the real magic lies within you. Your commitment to growth, learning, and application of these principles will determine the height of your achievements.

Manifestation is not merely a skill; it's an art form—one that you are now well-equipped to master. May your journey be filled with abundance, prosperity, and the joy of seeing your financial dreams manifest into reality. Happy manifesting!

PART VII
BONUS MATERIAL

SELF CONCEPT AFFIRMATIONS

SELF-CONCEPT AFFIRMATIONS FOR A MAGICAL LIFE

Welcome to a transformative journey toward embracing your most authentic and empowered self. Within this section of the book, you will discover a carefully curated collection of affirmations designed to reshape your self-concept and guide you toward living your most magical life. These affirmations are more than just words; they are seeds of intention, planted deep within the fertile soil of your subconscious mind, awaiting to sprout into your reality.

Before you begin, find a quiet space where you can be undisturbed. Make this practice a sacred ritual, performed each night before you drift into the world of dreams. As you repeat these affirmations out loud, visualize each word as a beam of light, illuminating the path toward your desired reality. Commit to this practice nightly for at least 21 days to allow your mind and body to fully align with these new beliefs.

- I now set an intention to be, do, and have all that I desire.
- I declare that everything in this universe is conspiring in my favor.
- I am a magnificent part of the divine.
- I am a powerful creative force.
- Divine energy flows through me uninterrupted every moment.
- I am a very important part of this universe.
- Whatever I desire comes to me quickly without any effort.
- My life experience is enriched with perfect ease and grace.
- I am limitless in every way.
- I am invincible.
- I now declare myself to be the luckiest person on this planet.
- My words have magnetic power, and everything I say becomes true in my reality.
- The universe blesses me in ways that I can never imagine.
- I am always loved and guided by the Divine.
- I am confident about myself and the path I want to pursue.

- I am calm, centered, and I know exactly what I want in life.
- I am very clear about all my life goals.
- I have a grand vision for my life.
- I take every step with complete faith in myself and the universe.
- I know that everything is working out for my highest good.
- I am in charge of how my life unfolds.
- I am creating my life experiences with the thoughts I think and the feelings I embody.
- I choose to think positively every day, no matter what.
- The outer circumstances have no power over me and my internal state.
- I am committed to my goals in every way.
- I only entertain thoughts and ideas that align with the future I want to create.
- I am naturally charismatic, and my magnetic aura attracts the right people into my life.
- I am always at the right place, at the right time, with the right people.
- I am loved and admired wherever I turn.
- Everyone who comes in contact with me is captivated by my strong presence and charm.
- I know my worth, so I never shy away from putting myself first.
- I am powerful beyond measure.
- I perceive every challenge as a divine opportunity to grow.
- I am fearless.
- I feel secure in my present and in my future.
- I love myself unconditionally.

- I deserve the very best the universe has to offer.
- I am ready to experience the absolute best in every area of my life.
- My life is filled with incredible wealth and riches.
- I am financially free, always.
- I have more than enough money to fulfill all my desires and goals.
- I have a stable and positive relationship with money.
- I have a healthy body and mind.
- Each cell of my body is brimming with vitality.
- I feel so good in my body, and I feel grateful for it.
- Every day my life is becoming more prosperous and fun.
- I am loving this human experience.
- While I enjoy the human experience, I never forget that I am much more than my physical body.
- I am an extension of the force that creates everything.
- It is my birthright to be highly successful at everything I do.
- I touch sand and it turns to gold, that's how lucky I am.
- Others are hypnotized by my charm and aura.
- I have an amazing personality.
- I radiate confidence and positivity.
- I accept myself for who I am, so I never seek validation from others.
- I am worthy of unconditional love.
- I now open my heart to attracting love into my life.
- My strong magnetic pull attracts the best people into my life.
- I am destined to live a life of bliss and wonderful companionship.

- I am a blessing to everyone who is a part of my life.
- I have everything that any person could desire.
- I am complete and content in my own existence.
- My relationship with my inner being is the strongest, and it is always my first priority.
- I have a solid spiritual connection with the source.
- I spend my days daydreaming about the wonderful future I am about to experience.
- I always stay in a state of wish fulfilled.
- I am always embodying the feelings of my desired future.
- I have become a master of creating my own reality.
- Whatever I want comes to fruition without any delay.
- I am a powerful manifester.
- People are amazed by how quickly my desires become a reality.
- The divine energy is always creating wonderful things through me.
- I am a genius.
- The universe inspires me with the right ideas and solutions.
- I am destined for greatness in every aspect of my life.
- I achieve everything I put my mind into.
- I am an abundant child of an abundant universe.
- There is more than enough of everything good and positive in this universe.
- It feels so good to be in charge of my own life circumstances.
- I enjoy this responsibility.
- I now give myself permission to live the life I have always wanted.

- All that I need to be successful is with me.
- I have every tool and resource at my disposal.
- My life is becoming even more beautiful every single day.
- My heart is bursting with joy and gratitude.
- I am very grateful for my blessings that are constantly multiplying.
- I now set an intention to go to sleep with these feelings of gratitude.
- As I will rest, my subconscious will be working to turn all my words into reality.
- Tomorrow is a new day, and I choose to start it with a positive mindset.
- Thank you, universe! Thank you, my inner being! Thank you, life!
- Thank you! Thank you! Thank you!

EMBRACING THE CHANGE

As you journey with these affirmations, visualize each one not just as a statement but as a declaration of your undeniable truth. Each repetition is a commitment to your growth, a step closer to manifesting your desires into your physical reality. Let the energy of gratitude infuse each word, for gratitude is the soil in which the seeds of your affirmations will bloom into the life you've always dreamed of.

Remember, this practice is a sacred dialogue between

you and the universe. With each affirmation, you are conversing with the cosmos, aligning your energy with the boundless abundance that awaits you. So, embark on this journey with an open heart and a willing spirit, and witness the transformation that unfolds.

AFFIRMATIONS FOR WEALTH & ABUNDANCE

WEALTH AND ABUNDANCE AFFIRMATIONS FOR MANIFESTING PROSPERITY

Within the fabric of reality, a thread of abundance weaves its magic, waiting for you to grasp it with both hands. This section is dedicated to reshaping your relationship with wealth, to teach you the art of attracting financial abundance effortlessly and joyfully. As Neville Goddard teaches, imagining creates reality, and through the power of affirmations, you can craft a life of limitless wealth and prosperity.

Before diving into these affirmations, create a sanctuary of peace for yourself where you can relax and fully engage with each statement. This practice is not just about recitation; it's an invitation to embody the essence of each affirmation, to feel its truth resonate within the core of your being. Commit to this practice nightly, before you sleep, for a continuous cycle of 21 days. This period allows your subconscious mind to soak in the new paradigm of wealth and abundance that you are choosing to live by.

AFFIRMATIONS FOR WEALTH AND PROSPERITY

- Being wealthy & successful is my birthright.
- I now open myself to unlimited amounts of wealth and prosperity.
- I am a channel for God's riches, and they flow through me uninterrupted.
- Everything in the universe aligns to give me exactly what I want.
- I have a healthy relationship with money.
- I love and appreciate the money that shows up in my experience.
- More and more wealth and riches are showing up in my life.
- I am smart and capable of achieving everything I desire.
- Everything I try, I end up becoming successful at it.
- Nothing is off-limits for me.
- I achieve all my life goals easily and effortlessly.
- I attract large amounts of money in my life on a regular basis.
- I now allow myself to receive incredible opportunities for money and success.
- I am always where I need to be.
- Positive shifts are happening in my life on a daily basis.
- My life is constantly becoming more enjoyable.

- I choose to trust the process.
- I let miracles unfold in my life.
- The universe provides me with all that I need and want.
- I have multiple income sources.
- Each source of income brings me an infinite amount of money.
- I understand that money is energy and must be approached with a positive mindset.
- I now align myself with the frequency of outrageous abundance.
- I experience abundance in all areas of my life.
- Each aspect of my life is filled with ease and happiness.
- I am the happiest person on this planet.
- I have all the right resources at my disposal.
- The powerful energy that creates worlds is now flowing through me and creating through me.
- I am an amazing creator.
- I am the architect of my own reality.
- I create the right changes in my life just by thinking the right thoughts.
- I always think positively.
- I always expect the best to happen to me, and only the best happens.
- I live a life of complete financial security.
- I live a life of luxury and opulence.
- I always have the resources to do anything I want.
- I now release all my money blocks.
- I release any resistance that might be keeping me from attracting money.
- I am capable of dealing with any challenges that come my way.

- I learn and grow with each challenge.
- I am becoming better and better at the game of life.
- I know how I can influence my own reality.
- The money I receive is a source of good for all.
- I attract the right clients and business opportunities.
- I effortlessly achieve all my money goals.
- I am becoming more affluent and more prosperous.
- My heart is open to the frequency of infinite abundance.
- I love and embrace the feeling of having more than enough money.
- I love the feeling of having more than enough money to help others.
- Each dollar I spend comes back to me multiplied.
- I say thank you whenever I spend money, and it always comes back to me in abundance.
- I am free of financial worries.
- I am unbelievably lucky with money.
- I am at ease while receiving money.
- Money comes into my life with multiple other blessings.
- My relationships are solid, and I have wonderful people in my life.
- I am loved and valued in all my relationships.
- Everyone I know loves and respects me.
- It feels so good to be genuinely appreciated by others.
- Every person in my life is a source of happiness and ease.
- I rejoice in my perfect health and well-being.
- My body and mind are becoming healthier by the day.
- I am becoming happier by the day.
- My mind is calm and serene.

- My mind is a receiver of great ideas from the divine.
- The universe gives me ideas about what adventures to undertake.
- I am guided by the divine force that creates everything.
- I am always protected in every way.
- The universe adores me and is watching over me every second.
- I am confident.
- I am full of bliss and joy.
- My perspective of looking at life circumstances is very optimistic.
- I see opportunities where others see challenges.
- I have mastered the art of turning challenges into beautiful opportunities.
- I am among the top 5% of the most successful people in the world.
- I do not shy away from my own greatness.
- I give myself permission to truly shine and thrive in every way.
- I now make an intention to be the very best I can be.
- I now make an intention to let in more money and comfort.
- I am ready to experience a fantastic future.
- I now embody the positive feelings of my future.
- I am creating my future, one thought at a time, one feeling at a time.
- The universe works to meet all my positive expectations every time.
- It's so easy to be rich and successful.
- It's easy to have a life filled with happiness and adventure.

• I love you, dear universe, and I thank you for all my blessings.

This collection of affirmations is a treasure trove, designed to transform your financial reality. As you embrace these affirmations, allow yourself to fully embody the feelings they evoke. With each repetition, envision your life transforming, aligning more closely with the abundance that is your birthright. Let gratitude be the foundation of this practice, for it is through gratitude that we open the door to endless possibilities.

GUIDED MEDITATION: LIVING YOUR BEST LIFE!

Choose a tranquil and comfortable space for this meditation. Sit with your spine straight, hands resting gently on your knees or thighs. Inhale deeply. Take another deep breath, hold it, and exhale slowly. Continue this breathing pattern once more, inhaling deeply, holding, and exhaling. Let's do it again: inhale deeply, hold, and exhale.

Focus your attention now on the top of your head. Notice any sensations there. Can you detect a vibration or a tingle? Consciously relax the muscles of your scalp, letting go of any tension. Move your awareness to your forehead, sensing any tingling or vibration. Gently tighten the muscles of your forehead, then release them, letting relaxation spread.

Shift your focus to your eyes, noting the sensation in and around them. Relax your eyebrows, eyelids, and every part of your eye area. Feel the relaxation deepen.

Now, bring your attention to your chin, jawline, and cheeks. Notice any sensations here and allow any tightness to dissolve as you relax these areas.

Turn your awareness to your back, feeling your spine. Allow relaxation to cascade down your back, relaxing each muscle from your neck down to your lower back. Gradually shift your focus to your arms, from shoulders to fingertips, allowing each part to relax fully.

Scan the front of your body next, from your chest down to your legs. Notice any sensations and allow your legs, knees, ankles, and feet to relax completely. Pay special attention to the sensations in your toes and feet, releasing any lingering tension.

With your body and mind now in a state of deep relaxation, you're ready for mental creation. Envision yourself having made a quantum leap into your desired future, where all your wishes have materialized. Picture your ideal living space—its warmth, the light streaming through windows, the comfort it provides.

See yourself in a mirror within this space. Observe your reflection—the texture of your skin, the look in your eyes, the state of your body. Embrace the feeling of health and satisfaction with your physical appearance.

Contemplate your financial situation. Imagine the abundance in your bank accounts, the sufficiency for a luxurious life. Visualize yourself engaged in your ideal professional activity, noting how much you earn and how it makes you feel.

Reflect on your relationships. Visualize the depth of love and connection you share with your partner and loved ones. Allow the feelings of joy, love, and contentment to fill you.

Spend a few moments combining all these elements into a vivid visualization of your perfect life. Immerse yourself in scenes of laughter, love, adventure, and fulfillment. Dream big, adding detailed textures to this vision of your best life.

As you conclude this visualization, acknowledge the successful imprinting of these desires on your subconscious. Prepare to return to your physical presence. I will count from five to one, and with each number, you'll become more aware of your surroundings.

Five... feel the energy returning to your body.
Four... become aware of the room around you.
Three... take a deep, energizing breath.
Two... start to move your fingers and toes.
One... when you're ready, return fully to the present moment, carrying the feelings of your envisioned future with you.

Congratulations on completing this meditation. You've taken a significant step toward manifesting your ideal future.

Carry this sense of fulfillment and readiness with you as you move forward in your day and life.

Printed in Great Britain
by Amazon